follower first

Rethinking Leading in the Church

RUSTY RICKETSON

Heartworks Publications
Cumming, Georgia

Heartworks Publications
2300 Bethelview Road Suite 110-248
Cumming, Georgia 30040

www.heartworkspublications.com

Printed in the United States of America

Library of Congress Cataloging-in-Publication Data

Ricketson, Rusty
      Follower First: Rethinking Leading in the Church /Rusty Ricketson
      Includes bibliographical references and index.
      ISBN : 978-0-9825332-0-8
         1.   Leadership
         2.   Christian leadership
         3.   Followership
         4.   Church Growth

Cover design by Copper Nelms - coppernelms@me.com

Dedication

To all who truly follow the Lord Jesus Christ and influence others to follow Him.

Appreciation

I am grateful to my family, my colleagues and students at Luther Rice Seminary & University, participants in the Follower First Conferences, and my fellow pastors and friends who have influenced and encouraged me to complete this work. Your input and participation with me in this project have taught me much about following Christ.

Contents

Introduction

I need to let you know that I am a recovering leader. My journey is not unlike countless thousands: graduate from college, work a job, graduate from seminary, serve a ministry, seek further education to try and become the best you can be at what God has called you to do. Somewhere along my journey, however, I stopped questioning what I was reading and began trying to find someone to tell me what would work in the ministry. The pressures of the pastorate and the internal and external demands to grow a church became my own personal pressure cooker. My thoughts changed from questioning whether or not the information I was reading was biblical to whether or not the information would be the magic pill that would solve the current struggle or at least transform me so that I could lead the ministry correctly.

When I finally began to read more critically, question the assumptions made by much of the leadership literature, and then compare these assumptions with the direct teachings of the Bible, I discovered a life-changing truth: **The Bible is a book about followers, written by followers, for followers.** The thrust of the Bible is not about leading or even teaching people how to become leaders. The Bible is about following and becoming the very best follower of Christ a Christian can be. The implication is simple, wherever the Lord may place me to lead others or to follow others; I am always a **Follower First**. This single truth has changed my entire perspective with regard to teaching leaders how to lead.

I hope to show that Christian leadership teaching that does not contain a Follower First philosophy misses an important theme that resonates throughout the Bible. The Bible certainly has much to say regarding leaders and leading. However, a good portion of the current Christian leadership literature appears to embrace a leader-centered philosophy that mirrors what is accepted within for-profit business organizational cultures rather than the follower theme of the Scriptures. In many instances it seems writers have simply taken popular business principles regarding leaders and leader theories and have sought to impose these theories and principles as a template on the text of Scripture. Instead of allowing the Bible to speak, we have muzzled its teaching by reading with a preconceived thought process that places being a leader and becoming a leader as the ultimate goal of the Christian life. I find no such teaching in the Old or New Testaments. I hope through reading this book you will begin to question your own leader presuppositions and begin to embrace the thinking that the ultimate goal of the believer is to be a follower of Christ *first*, regardless of organizational position.

As you read you will notice that except for explanation purposes I write more about leading and following than leadership or followership. This is due to my bias against *ships* and *isms* that we often create to try and make sense of various concepts. We talk of leadership, and followership, and discipleship, and evangelism, but these are terms we have created to help codify certain teachings into nice manageable constructs. The Bible, however, does not speak in terms of *ships* and *isms*. The Bible speaks of leaders and leading but not leadership. The Bible speaks of disciples and making disciples but not discipleship. For instance, we take the action verb *lead* with all its life and power and develop the verb into a noun making it a static construct made up of do's and don'ts. I believe the Lord intentionally wrote "make disciples," "do the work of an evangelist," and "follow Me," so that we would avoid codified *ships* and *isms* that have a tendency to produce organizational inertia by classifying normal Christian activity into specialized spiritual categories. Thus, our energies and organizations are side-tracked by recruiting church members to get involved in evangelism, discipleship, or leadership as we have defined these terms and neatly packaged them in 12 week courses for people to complete but not necessarily apply as a lifestyle. As a result, our churches are filled with people who have completed a course of study but see no connection of this teaching to daily life. This disconnect continues to create inertia in the church and be a major cause of her ineffectiveness.

I am really not a leadership kind of guy. When I use the term leadership, please understand I am referring to an intentional interdependence between both leaders and followers as the definition and not to individuals or positions. There are a few authors with whom I agree who posit that leadership is not solely vested in the leader as a person or in a leader's position, but is, rather, a process that includes interdependence between leaders and followers resulting in what we commonly recognize as leadership (one person influencing another person(s) to achieve a common goal). Without leaders and followers responding reciprocally with each other in positive ways, leadership never occurs, community within the church is never established, and the organization flounders. The church has leaders, but leadership occurs when the Body of Christ is submissive to the will of God within the context of each member's defined responsibility. I am for leaders and followers cooperating with each other within their God-given set of responsibilities.

I realize my thoughts may appear quixotic, idealistic, unrealistic, and impracticable to some. Being a follower, after all, is not a position to which anyone is taught to aspire, especially in American culture. I was told I needed to become a leader because, in the estimation of others, I had leader qualities. Society, authors, academia, and my own intuition agreed that being a leader was better than being a follower. All the books and leadership teachers stated with confidence that "everything rises or falls on leadership." The implied meaning being, if you want to really do something with your life you need to become a leader. Followers don't accomplish anything. Followers don't change the world. Followers don't influence anyone. Followers are necessary because without them we would have no leaders. The oft quoted Chinese proverb, "If you think you are leading and turning around find no one following, you are only taking a walk" is true, isn't it? We have all heard it time and again; being the leader is where the power and the influence are. In much of the leadership literature the prevailing thought regarding followers remains that people should avoid being a follower at all cost.

I challenge you to rethink what being a biblical leader entails. Are these axioms in the leadership literature actually true? I submit to you that the beginning point for any Christian leader in any organization, and especially the church, is to understand that because we are followers of Jesus Christ, organizationally, we are always to perceive ourselves as Followers First. I hope within the pages of this book you find an argument that will cause you to reconsider how leadership material is taught and implemented within the church. I also hope you will gain a new appreciation for what it means to be a follower. Far from being people who have no incentive, do not think for themselves, and only follow the crowd, believers with a Follower First philosophy think and act as competent individuals while submitting to the leading of Jesus Christ.

Chapter One studies the life of our Leader, Jesus Christ, and how through His purpose, commands, and teachings He declares Himself to be the perfect follower. Chapter Two investigates the need for Follower First thinking, especially in light of several unintended consequences that have occurred from leader-centered teaching. Chapter Three challenges the prevailing bias against followers evident in much of the current leadership literature and presents a different perspective on what being a follower entails. Chapter Four challenges the reader to develop his or her own follower identity. Chapter Five examines the idea of follower influence as it relates to power and control within the church. Chapter Six introduces the construct of the Following-Leader as a model for Christians to embrace within their organizations. Chapter Seven shares how a Follower First organizational culture can be embedded within the operation of a church. Chapter Eight seeks to identify follower first behaviors and introduces a measuring instrument, the Follower First Profile, with which to determine follower behaviors within the church. Finally, Chapter Nine closes the book by looking at the positive impact on the spread of the Gospel and the unified functioning within the local church that will result as churches embrace the responsibilities of a Follower First philosophy.

I understand the scope of such an undertaking is massive and that there is no possible way I can address all the various aspects of following and leading within this volume. This book is most definitely a work in progress. However, perhaps this work can serve as a catalyst to promote a conversation that needs to be had among those who write and practice leading and following within the church and organizations that have a Christian basis.

I realize my academic friends will be dissatisfied with some of my limited academic investigations. I also realize that my theological friends will question some of my assertions even though I believe I have stayed true to the text and context of Scripture. To all of you, I apologize in advance and only ask that you join in the conversation so that we all might discover the truth.

You will notice I refer to the church as an organization rather than an organism, a term some Christians use to describe the nature of the church. I do not disagree with the idea of the church being understood as a living entity because of the life of Christ within the individual members who make up the church. However, I refer to her as an organization because, from an organizational perspective, that is what the church is.

From my perspective, before the current concentration on leaders and leadership teaching, what the church thought was a crisis of leadership was actually a crisis of following. Now, however, after decades of teaching pastors how to be leaders we have compounded the problem. We still have not taught the followers of Christ how to follow within a church organization, and we now have a generation of leaders who think and act as leaders with little to no regard for being followers first. If the church is to make a change, it must begin with a biblical organizational understanding of following.

Now that you know my heart, I invite you to a new journey, a new way of thinking. I invite you to a new freedom, the freedom that comes from being a Follower First. I invite you to explore the possibility of building a bridge between laity and clergy and instigating greater church participation by teaching others that, even though we may have specific God-given roles within the church, we are all followers first. I urge you to consider the influence that can be had when God's people understand they don't have to be a leader or recognized as a leader to make a difference. As followers of Christ we can influence others while in the positions God gives whether those positions are perceived by society as being leadership positions or not, whether they have titles or not, whether they are paid positions or not. I invite you to see that throughout the Bible, God calls His people to follow. It is through following the commands of God that the people of God show their love for God and grow in their relationship with God (John 14:21). It is through following Christ we become "fishers of men" (Matthew 4:19). It is through following Christ we learn to "deny self, take up [our] cross daily, and follow [Him]" (Luke 9:23

Does this Follower First way of thinking resonate within you? Does concentrating on being a follower sound like something so radically counterintuitive to our current organizational way of thinking that it might be God's plan to change the world? Could it be that this Follower First way of thinking is what the church needs to make a greater impact on the culture as we begin this new century? From what I have studied in the Bible, I am thoroughly convinced that this impact will not come through robust, charismatic, larger-than-life leaders, but through faithful followers who, through the foolishness of following, influence others and actually become leaders in their own right. Still, the goal of followers is not to become leaders. The goal of followers is to be the very best followers they can be to the glory of God. And if these followers are placed in positions within companies, churches, or ministries in which they are responsible for others, their individual, primary understanding of their position will not be, "I am the leader." Their understanding will be:

I am a follower of Christ FIRST.

Others may call me a leader, but my primary understanding of my place on the planet is to be a follower of Christ, wherever He may lead.

The fulfillment of my life will not come from the praise of those whom I might lead in this lifetime.

**My goal and fulfillment in life will come when I hear, "Well done,"
from the lips of Him whom I have followed.**

Jesus said,

"If anyone serves Me, let him follow Me; and where I am, there My servant will be also. If anyone serves Me, him My Father will honor" (John 12:26).

Part I

Follow the Follower

Chapter 1

Jesus - The Perfect Follower

Conversing with Christian ministers and leaders throughout the United States, I find that many are searching for a way of thinking about leading that allows them to lead without succumbing to a type of CEO business model often presented by much of the Christian leadership literature. My personal observations are that ministers and Christian leaders want to know how to lead others effectively while thinking of themselves as leaders in a way that is consistent with the overall humility of the life of Christ, biblical teachings of humble service before God, and loving their neighbor. The Follower First philosophy fulfills this desire. The Follower First philosophy is compatible with much of the current teaching on becoming a leader and leading others and is also compatible with many leadership styles often suggested for Christian leaders to employ. The difference is that the Follower First philosophy does not emphasize what followers and leaders **do** as much as how leaders and followers **think of themselves** within an organization. If you are an organizational leader or follower, I want to challenge the way you think about who you are in the Body of Christ.

When I share with leaders the concepts of how being a Follower First leads to becoming a Following-Leader, it is as if a large weight is lifted from these leaders as they resonate with the scriptural congruence of the Follower First philosophy. I had one vice president of a large company share with me that he had been looking for a way to express his identity in Christ while working on the job and that the Follower First philosophy gives him greater courage to lead others as he follows Christ on the job. First time and veteran pastors also tell me that the Follower First philosophy gives them a new freedom to serve the church. This is the courage and freedom I hope all followers of Christ will find. However, what makes the Follower First philosophy a powerful force for change is its consistency with the life and teachings of Jesus Christ and other teachings of Scripture.

In most Christian leadership literature, the Lord Jesus Christ is often presented as the perfect leader. I certainly do not disagree with such an assertion. Jesus was, indeed, perfect in everything He did and said. I accept without question that when Jesus led others, He did so perfectly. However, from all that has been written regarding Jesus as a leader, one might begin to think that Jesus' purpose on the planet was to lead others. I would argue that the biblical evidence does not support such a claim. In fact, a close inspection of the biblical text, without the prevailing leader bias, reveals that Jesus' purpose, commands, and teachings were all centered on being a follower.

Jesus' Purpose

Jesus was the greatest follower who ever lived. At first blush such a statement might fly in the face of much of the literature that presents Jesus as the consummate leader. However, upon closer inspection, it was Jesus acting as a follower that influenced more people than His actual leading a small band of disciples. Consider Jesus stated purpose for being on the planet.

While proclaiming Himself to be the "bread of life" and that those who believe in Him will not be cast out, Jesus said,

> ...For <u>I have come down from heaven not to do my own will, but the will of Him who sent me.</u> This is the will of Him who sent Me, that of all He has given Me I should lose nothing but should raise it up at the last day (John 6:38, 39).

For our reflection, what is striking about this verse is Jesus' admission that His purpose was to follow the directives, the will, of His heavenly Father. From childhood, Jesus knew He "must be about [His] Father's business" (Luke 2:49). That business is beautifully portrayed in Philippians 2:5-11:

> Let this mind be in you which was also in Christ Jesus, who, being in the form of God, did not consider it robbery to be equal with God, but made Himself of no reputation, taking the form of a bondservant, and coming in the likeness of men. And being found in appearance as a man, He humbled Himself and became obedient to the point of death, even the death of the cross. Therefore God also has highly exalted Him and given Him the name which is above every name, that at the name of Jesus every knee should bow, of those in heaven, and of those on earth, and of those under the earth, and that every tongue should confess that Jesus Christ is Lord, to the glory of God the Father.

Although equal with God, Jesus "made Himself of no reputation." This translation does not give the full sense of Jesus emptying Himself as a direct translation of the Greek word *eknosen* requires.[1] The Amplified Bible translates the phrase "but stripped Himself [of all privileges and rightful dignity]." The NIV translates the verse, "but made himself nothing." All of these different translations seek to do justice to the concept that Jesus, although equal with God the Father, willingly humbled Himself and took the role of follower.

Jesus spoke of His follower status throughout His earthly ministry:

> John 5:30
> I can of Myself do nothing. As I hear, I judge; and My judgment is righteous, because I do not seek My own will but the will of the Father who sent Me.

> John 7:17-18
> If anyone wills to do His will, he shall know concerning the doctrine, whether it is from God or whether I speak on My own authority.

> John 12:49-50
> For I have not spoken on My own authority; but the Father who sent Me gave Me a command, what I should say and what I should speak.

> John 14:10-11
> Do you not believe that I am in the Father, and the Father in Me? The words that I speak to you I do not speak on My own authority; but the Father who dwells in Me does the works.

The Lamb of God, who takes away the sin of the world (John 1:29), was merely following what He had been directed by the Father to say and do. Jesus did **nothing** on his own authority. He was a follower. He is equal with the Father in His deity, yet, for the purpose of the Godhead, Jesus became the follower. The Father is not **better** than Jesus because Jesus is the follower. God the Father, God the Son, and God the Holy Spirit do not operate based upon a concept of which Person is better than the other because each is perfect. Rather, the Father, Son, and Holy Spirit, operate based upon an accepted role and responsibility.

An oversimplification of this role and responsibility may be stated thus:

- **The Father's role is to be the authority and to bring about His will for His good pleasure.**

  "...for it is God who works in you both to will and to do for *His* good pleasure" (Philippians 2:13). (See Ephesians 1:5,9)

- **The Son's responsibility is to follow the will of the Father.**

  "I have come down from heaven not to do my own will, but the will of Him who sent me"(John 6:38). (See Luke 22:42)

- **The Holy Spirit's responsibility is to follow the will of the Son.**

  "However, when He, the Spirit of truth, has come, He will guide you into all truth; for He will not speak on His own *authority, but whatever He hears He will speak; and He will tell you things to come. He will glorify Me, for He will take of what is Mine and declare it to you. All things that the Father has are Mine. Therefore I said that He will take of Mine and declare it to you"* (John 16:13-15).

Because Christ is the head of the church (Colossians 1:18), we may say that within the church no one is of any greater importance within the Body than anyone else. The Bible makes it clear that there is no designation in the church with regard to worth regardless of a person's ethnicity, gender, or background (Galatians 3:28). I believe the same is true organizationally in the church. No one is better or more important because he or she is deemed the leader. No one is a failure or less important because he or she is deemed a follower. Spiritually, we are all equal in that we are all sinners forgiven by the grace of God. Organizationally in the church we are all equal in that we are all followers. Even though we may be gifted differently, no one has meritorious rank or worth over any other person within the body of

21

Christ (1 Corinthians 12:12-31). The only ranking member of the Body of Christ is Christ Jesus. Any differentiation among members within the body comes at the level of the responsibilities we are called, gifted, and willing to assume. We will investigate this claim in Chapter 5.

We all have roles and responsibilities within the Body of Christ. Some church organizations and denominations may vest organizational authority in a particular person or persons in the church. However, this authority does not supersede that of Christ or the Bible and only extends to the individual(s) as the Scriptures allow. Thus, the beginning point of the effective functioning of the Body is an understanding that, under the leading of the Lord, **we are all followers.**

Jesus followed the will of the Father until the day He died. Yet, through His death and subsequent resurrection, Jesus became the Savior of the world, a fact that has influenced countless millions of people. The gospel message proclaims that God had a plan to redeem the world to Himself, and this plan was followed perfectly by His only begotten Son.

Jesus' Commands

"Follow Me" are two of the most powerful words in the New Testament. With these words Jesus interjected Himself into the lives of others, and those who responded in the affirmative had their lives changed forever. Such a phenomenon is still true today. The power of these words leaves no room for doubt in the minds of those who hear them. The implication is clear, Jesus is offering an opportunity to be in relationship with Him. The clarity of the words can be seen in the literal understanding of the Greek word *akoloutheo,*[2] meaning to walk in the way with another. This particular Greek word was uttered by Jesus as an imperative on eight different occasions. When Jesus uttered the words "follow Me," He was not giving an invitation. He was giving a command.

An interesting historical side note is that as a rabbi, Jesus did not gather His disciples as other rabbis had done up until that time. Historically, rabbis would teach, and those who longed to follow would simply inform the rabbi that they were willing to sit under his teaching. Jesus, however, went a step further. There were those who followed

Jesus and sat under His teaching according to the common practice of the time. However, for those whom Jesus wanted closest to Him, these individuals would have to respond to His command, "Follow Me."

When we look at these instances in the New Testament, it almost appears that Jesus is deliberately issuing this command to the most unlikely group of people you would want to be on your leadership team. I believe the reason for this is quite simple. Jesus was not looking for leaders. **Jesus was looking for followers.** Let us consider these eight instances in which Jesus commanded someone to "Follow Me."

Philip

John 1:43-49
The following day Jesus wanted to go to Galilee, and He found Philip and said to him, "Follow Me." Now Philip was from Bethsaida, the city of Andrew and Peter. Philip found Nathanael and said to him, "We have found Him of whom Moses in the law, and also the prophets, wrote — Jesus of Nazareth, the son of Joseph." And Nathanael said to him, "Can anything good come out of Nazareth?" Philip said to him, "Come and see." Jesus saw Nathanael coming toward Him, and said of him, "Behold, an Israelite indeed, in whom is no deceit!" Nathanael said to Him, "How do You know me?" Jesus answered and said to him, "Before Philip called you, when you were under the fig tree, I saw you." Nathanael answered and said to Him, "Rabbi, You are the Son of God! You are the King of Israel!"

When Jesus commanded Phillip, "Follow Me," Phillip immediately found Nathanael. Having accepted the position as a follower of Christ, Philip influenced others to become followers as well. Are such actions indicative of those within our churches who claim to follow Christ?

The Exceptional Disciple

Matthew 8:18-22
And when Jesus saw great multitudes about Him, He gave a command to depart to the other side. Then a certain scribe came

and said to Him, "Teacher, I will follow You wherever You go." And Jesus said to him, "Foxes have holes and birds of the air have nests, but the Son of Man has nowhere to lay His head." Then another of His disciples said to Him, "Lord, let me first go and bury my father." But Jesus said to him, "Follow Me, and let the dead bury their own dead."

Although these words appear to be harsh, Jesus uses them to teach a key truth regarding being a follower of Christ. Christ must be preeminent in our lives and in our churches and organizations (Colossians 1:18). Our relationship with and to Him takes precedent over every other relationship. We cannot afford to be distracted by good things at the expense of following Him.

Matthew

Matthew 9:9 (Mark 2:14; Luke 5:27)
As Jesus passed on from there, He saw a man named Matthew sitting at the tax office. And He said to him, "Follow Me." So he arose and followed Him.

In my mind's eye I can almost see the shock on Matthew's face as he is confronted by Jesus and challenged by the words "Follow Me." I can imagine Matthew might have looked around to make certain Jesus was talking to him and then pointed to himself as if to say, "Who me?" For Jesus to have approached a hated tax collector was a total contradiction of societal norms. Matthew certainly must have been stigmatized by many. Perhaps one of the lessons we can learn from this encounter is that no one, even the most despised, is disqualified from being a follower of Christ.

Potential Disciples

Matthew 16:24-27
Then Jesus said to His disciples, "If anyone desires to come after Me, let him deny himself, and take up his cross, and follow Me. For whoever desires to save his life will lose it, but whoever

loses his life for My sake will find it. For what profit is it to a man if he gains the whole world, and loses his own soul? Or what will a man give in exchange for his soul? For the Son of Man will come in the glory of His Father with His angels, and then He will reward each according to his works.

We will discuss this verse in more detail in a later chapter. For now, let it suffice to say that Jesus understands there are certain behaviors which characterize His followers. As followers, we are to deny self, take up our cross, and follow Him. If our behaviors do not culminate in following Him, then all of our religious activities are for nothing.

The Rich Young Ruler

Matthew 19:16-22
Now behold, one came and said to Him, "Good Teacher, what good thing shall I do that I may have eternal life?" So He said to him, "Why do you call Me good? No one *is* good but One, *that is,* God. But if you want to enter into life, keep the commandments." He said to Him, "Which ones?" Jesus said, "*'You shall not murder,' 'You shall not commit adultery,' 'You shall not steal,' 'You shall not bear false witness,' 'Honor your father and your mother,'* and, *'You shall love your neighbor as yourself.'*" The young man said to Him, "All these things I have kept from my youth. What do I still lack?" Jesus said to him, "If you want to be perfect, go, sell what you have and give to the poor, and you will have treasure in heaven; and come, follow Me." But when the young man heard that saying, he went away sorrowful, for he had great possessions.

I find it interesting that the one person who appears on the surface to have all the qualifications for leadership is the one person who refused to obey the compassionate command of Jesus. Perhaps we might think twice before we invest too much in outward appearances, achievements, personality, and social position when finding leaders for the church. This man may have made an excellent leader. He obviously had riches and was a successful businessman. In leader-centered churches it is possible that such a person could become a deacon or an elder. **It may be that all too often we have looked for leaders, when what we should be looking for are followers of Christ. This rich young ruler may have been a leader among his peers, but he refused to be a follower of Christ to his own peril.**

The Servant

> John 12:23-26
> But Jesus answered them, saying, "The hour has come that the Son of Man should be glorified. Most assuredly, I say to you, unless a grain of wheat falls into the ground and dies, it remains alone; but if it dies, it produces much grain. He who loves his life will lose it, and he who hates his life in this world will keep it for eternal life. <u>If anyone serves Me, let him follow Me;</u> and where I am, there My servant will be also. If anyone serves Me, him My Father will honor.

Of all the characterizations of Jesus, the idea of the suffering servant is one that strikes at the heart of His character and behavior. The idea of service is so pronounced in the scriptures that Jesus even said that the one who would be the greatest would be the servant of all (Mark 9:35). Servant Leadership is often touted as the biblical leadership theory. From a biblical perspective the theory does have merit. But let us not forget that according to this verse, if we are to serve Christ we must follow Him. Jesus does not say if anyone follows me let him serve Me. We cannot claim to serve Christ if we are not following Him. Additionally, it is important to note that the one who seeks to **follow and serve** the Lord Jesus is the one whom the Father will honor.

Peter's Restoration

> John 21:17-19
> He said to him the third time, "Simon, son of Jonah, do you love Me?" Peter was grieved because He said to him the third time, "Do you love Me?" And he said to Him, "Lord, You know all things; You know that I love You." Jesus said to him, "Feed My

sheep. Most assuredly, I say to you, when you were younger, you girded yourself and walked where you wished; but when you are old, you will stretch out your hands, and another will gird you and carry you where you do not wish." This He spoke, signifying by what death he would glorify God. And when He had spoken this, He said to him, "Follow Me."

There is no more beautiful expression of love and intimacy than that between Peter and the Lord Jesus during this time of restoration. Three times Peter denied the Lord Jesus, and three times Jesus pressed upon Peter his responsibility to feed and tend the followers of Christ. Additionally, Jesus loved Peter enough to let him know by what type of death Peter would glorify God. The path to that God glorifying death was through Jesus' command, "Follow Me."

Peter's Rebuke

John 21:20-22
Then Peter, turning around, saw the disciple whom Jesus loved following, who also had leaned on His breast at the supper, and said, "Lord, who is the one who betrays You?" Peter, seeing him, said to Jesus, "But Lord, what about this man?" Jesus said to him, "If I will that he remain till I come, what is that to you? You follow Me."

It takes all of perhaps one minute for Peter to take his eyes and thoughts off following the Lord and start concerning himself with what others might do. Jesus' rebuke is clear and to the point. In essence Jesus says to Peter, it does not matter what I have planned for John, you are to follow ME.

How often do we allow the thought of what others might say or what others are doing to affect our obedience to follow Christ? As a pastor, I was often tempted to compare my ministry to that of another. Such comparisons always resulted in my either becoming proud because I was comparing my church with another that was not doing as well or my becoming depressed when comparing my church with another that was growing much faster. Either way, such comparisons were not healthy. All of us within the church would do well to avoid comparisons with others and concentrate on comparing our lives and our churches with that of Christ and His commands.

A Different Word

Peter and Andrew Called

Perhaps the most well known "Follow-Me" imperative of Jesus is when He called Peter and Andrew.

Matthew 4:19
"Follow Me and I will make you to become fishers of men."

The Greek word used in this exchange is different from the previous imperative. Here the word is *deute opisow* meaning "come after."[3] The word has the idea of lining up after someone. This word for *come* is spoken to those who labor and are heavy laden (Matthew 11:28-30), to those invited to the marriage supper (Matthew 22:4-5), by the woman at the well to summon others to meet Jesus (John 4:29), and nine other occasions in the New Testament.[4]

What is striking about this encounter between Jesus and Peter and Andrew is Jesus' direct manner with which He interjects Himself into these men's normal activity. A second feature of the command is the explanation of what they will be about after following Jesus. They well become "fishers of men." Finally, one is struck by the immediate response of the two fishermen. The Bible records that they "immediately dropped their nets and followed Him." Such is the power of the Lord's, "Follow Me." The subsequent calling of James and John (Matthew 4:21) is indicative of the same response of those whom Jesus called. They immediately left their nets and their father and followed Jesus.

Perhaps now would be a good time to reflect upon our own responses when we hear the Lord's, "Follow Me." Are we willing for the Lord to interrupt our daily lives, our routines, our comfort zones? Is there any delay between reading the Lord's command from the Bible and our response? Are we asking God to enable us through His Spirit to immediately respond? Such questions may lead us to a greater appreciation for these disciples and a greater desire to imitate their following after the Lord.

Jesus' Teaching

When we listen to the teachings of Jesus from a follower's perspective, we recognize His authority loudly and clearly. At the same time, Jesus' teaching centers not on developing leadership skills and traits but concentrating on a relationship with Him. Leading others results from this relationship of following Christ in all things.

Worthy Followers

Matthew 10:37-39
He who loves father or mother more than Me is not worthy of Me. And he who loves son or daughter more than Me is not worthy of Me. And he who does not take his cross and follow after Me is not worthy of Me. He who finds his life will lose it, and he who loses his life for My sake will find it.

It is sometimes difficult for us to believe that Jesus would actually place a worth on following after Him. But within this context there is no denying Jesus' plain teaching that only those who know how to carry out a daily dying to self (we will talk more about this in a later chapter) and placing as the most important aspect of life a relationship with Christ are worthy of being in relationship with Him.

My Sheep Follow

John 10:25-30
Jesus answered them, "I told you, and you do not believe. The works that I do in My Father's name, they bear witness of Me. But you do not believe, because you are not of My sheep, as I said to you. My sheep hear My voice, and I know them, and

they follow Me. And I give them eternal life, and they shall never perish; neither shall anyone snatch them out of My hand. My Father, who has given them to Me, is greater than all; and no one is able to snatch them out of My Father's hand. I and My Father are one."

The above verses are some of the more endearing passages of all Scripture. Jesus stated that His sheep hear His voice. Jesus also said that He knows these sheep, and these sheep have a specific activity; they follow Him. These sheep count it their greatest comfort to follow Jesus.

You Will Follow

John 13:36
Simon Peter said to Him, "Lord, where are You going?" Jesus answered him, "Where I am going you cannot follow Me now, but you shall follow Me afterward

Prior to His crucifixion, death, and resurrection, Jesus sought to prepare His disciples with these words. The disciples had followed Jesus for years. However, now there would be a separation. They would not be allowed to follow: "…you cannot…." However, the promise is extended that they would be allowed to "…follow Me afterward." The entire idea of relationship after Jesus' death, burial and resurrection is couched in terms of following.

Those Who Will Not Follow

Luke 6:39-41
And He spoke a parable to them: "Can the blind lead the blind? Will they not both fall into the ditch? A disciple is not above his teacher, but everyone who is perfectly trained will be like his teacher."

In this instance Jesus is referring to leaders who do not follow. They are incapable of following because they are blind. The Pharisees thought themselves leaders in the community because of their great knowledge and adherence to the Law. Jesus recognizes their positions of leadership. However, what does it profit anyone if the leader cannot see?

From a follower perspective there is no such thing as blindly following leaders because they happen to hold an organizational or societal position as leaders. Followers follow those whom they know follow the Lord Jesus Christ. A point for all to remember is that if you want to know where your leader is going and how he plans to treat you along the way, find out who or what the leader is following, and you will know both where he is going and how you can expect to be treated. If your leader is following fame and fortune and prestige and money, then you can expect to be treated as a commodity or a stepping-stone in the leader's career. However, if the leader follows the Lord, you can expect to be treated with the respect a follower has for God's human creation. This spirit of mutual respect is a ubiquitous characteristic of those who hold to a Follower First philosophy.

Conclusion

The Bible is clear that Jesus came to follow, call followers, and follow the will of the Father through His life, teaching, death, and resurrection. In the future, Jesus will follow the will of the Father in His second coming (Mark 13:32). The thread of following the Lord is woven throughout the Old and New Testament Scriptures. As following the will of the Father was the purpose and teaching of the Lord Jesus Christ, so ministers and leaders within the church need to begin with a Follower First philosophy as we follow the "head of the church" (Ephesians 5:23).

By concentrating on being a faithful follower, ministers will be able to seek their "well done" from the Lord Jesus rather than from their peers, or denominations, or self. This new freedom will provide a greater motivation to learn to lead from a follower perspective and trust in the enabling and leading of the Holy Spirit more than the often mechanistic practices prescribed by some. Follower First thinking will allow ministry leaders the opportunity to reassess how much the follower with responsibilities (minister, elder, deacon, church member) in the church really is dependent on the Lord. It will help all see more clearly how God glorifies Himself through the "foolish things of the world" (1 Corinthians 1:27).

Think of Jesus' disciples. Who were they? There was never assembled a more eclectic bunch of losers in the history of mankind. The Bible is silent with regard to why Jesus called these men to "Follow Me." Any conjecture regarding Jesus seeing leadership potential in these men is simply that: conjecture. One truth we do know is these men were Jesus' first followers. The Apostle Paul captured the essence of all true leaders and followers in the church when he said:

For ye see your calling, brethren,
how that not many wise men after the flesh,
not many mighty,
not many noble,
are called:
But God hath chosen the foolish things of the world
to confound the wise; and
God hath chosen the weak things of the world
to confound the things which are mighty;
And base things of the world,
and things which are despised,
hath God chosen,
yea, and things which are not,
to bring to naught things that are:
That no flesh should glory in his presence.
But of him are ye in Christ Jesus,
who of God is made unto us wisdom, and righteousness, and
sanctification, and
redemption:
That, according as it is written,
He that glorieth, let him glory in the Lord.
(1 Corinthians 1:26-31)

Jesus: The Perfect Follower

Purpose – John 6:38

                  Role of the Trinity

Commands –

- Follow Me
- Jesus was looking for followers.
- 8 Imperatives - akoloutheo – *"walk in the way with another" (A command)*
  - Philip
  - The Exceptional Disciple
  - Matthew
  - Potential Disciples
  - The Rich Young Ruler
  - The Servant
  - Peter's Restoration
  - Peter's Rebuke
- A different word – deute opisow *"come after"*
  - Peter and Andrew *line up after*

Teaching

- Worthy Followers
- My Sheep Follow
- You will follow
- Those who will not follow

Chapter 2

Life from a
Follower Perspective

Enormous amounts of time, effort, and money have been concentrated on leaders, leadership, and leading. As a result, church practitioners, academics, and theoreticians have all but forgotten the followers who faithfully fulfill the work of the ministry and deserve our respect and understanding. My study of follower/leader relationships has brought me to the place where I can confidently say that the church's obsession with leadership has blinded her to a problem she does not want to recognize, because to do so, she has to admit that many current standard operating principles and methods are inconsistent with a *biblical* understanding of how Christ's church should function. Adopting non-biblically based methodologies has resulted in many churches becoming dysfunctional and ineffectively impacting their local communities and the culture at large. Much of the current leadership literature precipitates the acceptance of these aberrant systems by elevating becoming a leader as the optimal goal of the Christian life while forgetting, if not ignoring, the multitude of biblical texts calling for a faithful following of Christ as the primary operating principle. Instead of creating a unique organization with a unique purpose, this concentration on the organization's top few creates churches which establish leader-centered organizations functioning in similar fashion to for-profit businesses. What is needed is a way to perform the business of the church without becoming a church business.

I propose that we view the church from the perspective of the follower. When you read the Bible with a follower mindset, you will be astonished to find a large number of scriptures referencing the role and function of followers within the Body of Christ. Whether people find themselves in positions of leading or positions of following, the Bible is quite clear that they are to always think of themselves as followers.

There is no question the church needs good leaders. However, leaders need to be taught how to lead from a Follower First perspective, while followers need to follow from a Follower First perspective. The church is the most unique organization on the planet. Her Head, the Lord Jesus Christ, is physically absent but present through the indwelling Holy Spirit. The guidelines for church operation are given in the Bible, and our Head expects His church to fulfill them with the singular purpose of glorifying God in all that she does. Yet, it appears that operating with a leader-centered philosophy, rather than a Follower First philosophy results in the church experiencing many unintended consequences.

Unintended Consequences

Leaders are a necessary part of the church organization, and these leaders need to know how to lead. To support my argument for a more follower-centered perspective, I offer four specific unintended consequences that appear to have occurred during the past two decades of teaching a leader-centered approach: (a) church ineffectiveness, (b) member non-participation, (c) church divisions, and (d) cavalier biblical interpretations.

Church Ineffectiveness
One of the more popular sayings among leadership enthusiasts is, "Everything rises or falls on leadership." The statement implies that if leaders don't do the right things at the right time, then nothing is

accomplished. Statements such as this place leaders as the key figures in the organization who ultimately determine the success or failure of that organization. If it is true that "Everything rises or falls on leadership," then we might assume that the church has benefitted from over two decades of teaching on leadership and how to become leaders. Church statistics, however, do not support such an assumption.[1]

The Southern Baptist Convention, the largest Protestant denomination in the United States, reports that since 1950, the annual growth rate of Southern Baptist churches has been declining from an annual growth rate of 4.5% in 1950 to .5% today.[2] The United Methodist Church, the second largest protestant denomination in the United States, reports that Methodist churches experienced a 5.86% decrease in church membership from 1995 to 2005.[3] These statistics and those from other denominations indicate that church growth in the United States has slowed significantly.

Certainly there are many contributing factors to these disturbing statistics. However, if we accept the idea that everything rises or falls on leadership, then the leaders of these churches are to be held responsible for this decline. Leadership enthusiasts might conclude that leaders in these churches are not leading as they ought and need more training on how to motivate their members to obey the Great Commission. However, what if within the church organizational context everything does not rise or fall with leaders? What if God designed the church in such a way that followers, not just leaders, are held responsible for the growth of the church?

I suggest that the responsibility for this lack of church growth and impact on our communities is not primarily due to a lack of leaders or a lack of leadership skills. To assert that the primary reason for church stagnation rests with the pastor's lack of leadership is to offer too simplistic a view of the problem and also reveals a lack of understanding that the church is composed of followers with specific responsibilities. The church is an organized group of followers. If we are to levy any blame for this stagnation, the blame falls squarely with the followers of Christ within these congregations, whether they have positions of leadership or not. When Jesus said, "All authority has been given to Me in heaven and on earth. Go therefore and make disciples of all nations, baptizing them in the name of the Father and the Son and the Holy Spirit, teaching them to observe all that I commanded you; and lo, I am with you always, even to the end of the age" (Matthew 28: 18-20), He intended His words to apply just as much to followers of Christ who hold no leadership positions in the church as those followers who do hold positions of leadership. With a Follower First philosophy, followers of Christ within the church do not need someone to motivate them to do what the actual Leader of the church, Jesus, commands them to do. A Follower First philosophy teaches that followers do not have an option of whether or not they obey the commands of Christ simply because the follower does not like a particular pastor, elder, deacon, or teacher who is responsible for them. A Follower First philosophy encourages followers to fulfill the obvious commands of Christ, the Leader, whether the titular leader in the church is appreciated or not. However, such a philosophy of following is rarely found in today's church and results in a second unintended consequence.

Member Non-participation

For years the church has operated under the assumption of the 80/20 rule. Twenty percent of the people do the work while eighty percent sit on the sideline. There is not a pastor or church worker alive who has not experienced this phenomenon. I am certain those who were teaching leadership principles in the church had the desire to increase the twenty percent and reduce the eighty percent. However, my observations and interviews with church members and ministers indicate what many think increase the numbers of people participating in the church actually has a numbing effect on the church membership. By emphasizing leadership and everyone in the church becoming a leader, these leader-centered organizations subconsciously teach those *not* in positions of leadership and those who do not see themselves as ever becoming leaders that they are insignificant.

When the leaders only train potential leaders, a subconscious self-fulfilling prophesy begins. The leaders teach that leaders get things done and, as a result, those who are deemed non-leaders wait on the leaders to get things done. Unknowingly the leaders create an organization in which followers are reinforced to believe they have no initiative, no input, and no influence to make a difference. Non-leaders are relegated to the pejorative status of *follower*. As followers, these people have no say in any matter and may even develop an entitlement mentality. These followers are *sheep* and are expected to do what they are told. The role of the follower is subjugated to that of a barnyard animal that needs to submit to those who have leader responsibilities. Similarly, those who have leader responsibilities begin to think that if followers only knew their place and submitted to the church leaders everything would be wonderful. Such an attitude does not comprehend the biblical concept of followers.

The greatest impetus to the inactivity of the church and hindrance to participation in the church is the negative thinking of those who are members of the church. Emphasizing leadership and only training leaders with the attitude that leaders are the only ones who count has had little impact on the 80/20 rule. As a result, growing churches still need workers, current workers grow more and more tired, and the vast majority of people become more content to show up, sit for an hour, put a ten dollar tip in the offering plate, and then head to the restaurant and an afternoon of play. Such actions are commonplace because followers have not been taught the importance of following as a member of the church organization. The vast majority of followers are unaware how they influence those around them either positively or negatively. The continuous drumming of leadership drowns out any occasional appeal to the importance of the body to do the work of the ministry.

Church leaders may be charged with "equipping the saints to do the work of the ministry" (Ephesians 4:11), but the prevailing idea in some circles seems to be that the only saints worth equipping are those the current leaders think will one day become leaders. Who can fault the young follower of Christ for thinking that he or she doesn't have what it takes to really make a difference when they are not tapped for leadership training? The result is continued non-participation and the development of a wrong attitude on the part of the follower to let the leaders initiate and maintain all activities.

Church Divisions

One of the subtle demoralizing aspects of church organization is qualifying people into different categories of service within the church. When we use the word disciple or discipleship in our modern context, we give people the impression that they have to rise to a different level of Christian development.[4] Discipleship is often perceived as a higher level of spirituality. Most Christians do not perceive themselves as being spiritual people. They reserve that attribution for ministers who are called to full-time ministry. Church members determine that somewhere in that calling to vocational ministry these called individuals are somehow better Christians, better disciples, and better followers than the other regular, normal people (I resist the term lay people.) in the church.

In our churches we have come to the place where those who do spiritual things (witness, study the Bible, pray, have a quiet time) are labeled disciples. Those who do not are just Christians. We coin our phrase *discipleship* to identify processes by which Christians become disciples. However, this idea of disciples being substantively different than Christians is actually the reverse order of what we see in Scripture. The followers of Christ, the disciples, were first called Christians in Antioch (Acts 11:26). We believers are very good at comparing ourselves with ourselves and creating categories of spirituality to make ourselves feel better about ourselves. We don't want to be just Christians. We certainly don't want to be just followers. We want to be disciples. Of course, we leave it to ourselves to assess other people's discipleship quotients. We think, if you read your Bible as much as me, or pray as much as me, or worship as much as me, you might be a disciple too. Such assessments create division in the Body of Christ and have the potential of harboring pride, arrogance, and thoughts of superiority. Additionally, by creating discipleship we can separate the process of discipleship from evangelism and make ourselves feel better about our lack of sharing the gospel with others by saying we are not into evangelism but are more interested in discipleship. Such terminology creates a divisiveness that permeates the Body. In the same way, choosing to value leaders and devalue followers only exacerbates the division. We inadvertently develop leper colonies of people who are *just followers* because they do not measure up to our standards of what a leader ought to be.

Followers are well aware of their apparent lack of value to leaders. As a result, false divisions of the *haves* and the *have nots* occur creating a lack of unity and diminishing the corporate impact of the church.

A biblical understanding of following the person and teachings of Jesus Christ alleviates such pseudo divisions. With a Follower First perspective, because you follow Christ, you study the Bible (John 14:21). If you do not study the Bible, you do not follow Christ. Because you follow Christ, you share Him with others as a natural part of life (Matthew 18:18-20). If you do not, you do not follow Christ. From the follower perspective there is no debate, no caveat, no rationalizing. The church needs to quit qualifying itself into mediocrity. We are either followers of the Person and teachings of Jesus Christ and Scripture, or we are not.

The Follower First philosophy creates an atmosphere in the church where each person, regardless of position or title, recognizes others as fellow followers. Such thinking establishes a common ground of respect and understanding. With a Follower First philosophy, leaders think only of how to follow the Lord by serving and fulfilling their responsibility within the body. Those who are in positions of responsibility over others do not perceive themselves as being better, or special, or of more value than any other person in the Body of Christ. Followers are also aware of their role and responsibility to support their leaders as these leaders follow Christ. There is no jealousy or envy on the part of these Follower First followers. They understand and submit to the Scriptures and operate willingly under the godly leading of their leaders as together they follow the will of the Head, the Lord Jesus Christ.

Cavalier Interpretations

I have a great deal of respect for those who have written on the important concept of leading in the church. There is a wealth of good material available. However, the church needs to question the axioms, suppositions, assumptions, and principles of what some present as

41

teachings related to biblical leadership. If followers of Christ are not careful, they may partake in a leadership meal composed mostly of a gracious helping of business leader and management principles coupled with a small side dish of Bible verses, many of which are taken out of context. It concerns me when the church does not critically assess the biblical truth of a matter and carelessly consumes philosophies that have no place in the organization and operation of the Bride of Christ. I confess my bias is that although the church is an organization, it is the most unique organization on the planet. The church is operated by people, but these people supposedly have had something life-changing take place within them so that they are not conformed to the world's ways of operating (Romans 12:1-2). The church should be seen as a special organization, with a special purpose, operating with specific guidelines, and led by people transformed through a relationship with Jesus Christ. These characteristics are why the church must not fall prey to the idea that if a principle works within a business environment such a principle should be automatically enacted within the church without first determining the biblical validity of the principle. This is not to say that we cannot learn from extra biblical sources. The principle of general revelation allows us the opportunity to learn from other sources outside the Bible.[5] However, these social science and business sources should never be considered equal with, much less superior to, the authority of Scripture. The church must diligently reject leadership principles that contradict the Scriptures and scrutinize leadership principles based upon Scriptures that are taken out of context.

We can learn much from the way Jesus interacted with people. However, we must be careful not to make the actions of the Savior support any of our own preconceived ideas, especially such banal ideas as leadership. We must not allow the perfect life, death, and resurrection of the Lord Jesus Christ to become merely an "example" for us to follow. Nowhere in the New Testament is there didactic teaching from Jesus about how anyone should lead. All such leadership principles gleaned from His life are merely anecdotal and should be understood as being **descriptive, not prescriptive**.

There is no question that Jesus was the perfect leader and we can learn much from studying His actions. Being a perfect man, Jesus would have possessed every possible leadership quality, trait, and style. However, we should be careful not to cherry-pick events in Jesus' life to support our preconceived leadership principles. If we look at the life of Jesus we must look at His life as a whole. If Jesus was the perfect leader, then it follows that everything Jesus did with His followers was perfect and should be emulated as a leadership principle. Such a position does pose a problem with some of the more unique actions Jesus took with His disciples.

The leadership books are silent with regard to the Jesus leadership principle of, *Call Your Closest Associates Satan.*

> Then Peter took Him aside and began to rebuke Him, saying, "Far be it from You, Lord; this shall not happen to You!" but He turned and said to Peter, "Get behind Me, Satan! You are an offense to Me, for you are not mindful of the things of God, but the things of men" (Matthew 16:22-23).

I do not think any of today's leadership authorities would promote rebuking an associate with the words, "Get behind me Satan." This is not to say that we might have, on occasion, thought of such a rebuke. However, note the reason for Jesus' rebuke. Jesus points out that Peter was thinking from a human, selfish perspective, not God's perspective. Jesus' purpose on the planet was to glorify God, and His death on the cross would be the culmination of His life of perfect obedience. If we give Peter the benefit of the doubt we can say that his response was motivated by a love for Jesus, and he did not want to see Him die. However, Jesus could not allow Peter's love to stand in the way of the Father's glory. Human approval does not trump the will of God. In similar fashion, we cannot allow our study of leadership, or our study of following for that matter, to become a man-centered enterprise that only human beings approve. There must be a solid, exegetical basis for all our teaching, not simply the approval of others or the seeming success of certain leadership principles.

How often have we read the Jesus leadership principle of, *Destroy the Livelihood and Businesses of Your Opponents*?

> Now the Passover of the Jews was at hand, and Jesus went up to Jerusalem. And He found in the temple those who sold oxen and sheep and doves, and the money changers doing business. When He had made a whip of cords, He drove them all out of the temple, with the sheep and the oxen, and poured out the changers' money and overturned the tables. And He said to those who sold doves, "Take these things away! Do not make My Father's house a house of merchandise!" Then His disciples remembered that it was written, *"Zeal for Your house has eaten Me up"* (John 2:13-17).

Making a cord and whipping the merchants and money changers out of the temple is not the type of executive behavior we want our church leaders to manifest, or is it? Jesus' actions here, although appearing antisocial, were certainly within the will of the Father and consistent with Jesus' one desire to honor God the Father. Perhaps having leaders in the church who know how to recognize deceit, fraud, and manufactured worship is exactly what we need. We need leaders who manifest Jesus' passion for the honor of God the Father so that our churches don't become commercial centers for the selling of the gospel. To date, I have not seen anything written with regard to this particular leadership event in the life of Jesus.

One other leadership principle that often gets overlooked is *Go to Parties with Scoundrels and Prostitutes.*

> Jesus said, "The Son of Man has come eating and drinking; and you say, 'Behold, a gluttonous man, and a drunkard, a friend of tax-gatherers and sinners!' Yet wisdom is vindicated by all her children."
>
> Now one of the Pharisees was requesting Him to dine with him. And He entered the Pharisee's house, and reclined at the table. And behold, there was a woman in the city who was a sinner; and when she learned that He was reclining at the table in the Pharisee's house, she brought an alabaster vial of perfume, and standing behind Him at His feet, weeping, she began to wet His feet with her tears, and kept wiping them with the hair of her head, and kissing His feet, and anointing them with the perfume.

Now when the Pharisee who had invited Him saw this, he said to himself, "If this man were a prophet He would know who and what sort of person this woman is who is touching Him, that she is a sinner." And Jesus answered and said to him, "Simon, I have something to say to you." And he replied, "Say it, Teacher." "A certain moneylender had two debtors: one owed five hundred denarii, and the other fifty. "When they were unable to repay, he graciously forgave them both. Which of them therefore will love him more?" Simon answered and said, "I suppose the one whom he forgave more." And He said to him, "You have judged correctly." And turning toward the woman, He said to Simon, "Do you see this woman? I entered your house; you gave Me no water for My feet, but she has wet My feet with her tears, and wiped them with her hair. "You gave Me no kiss; but she, since the time I came in, has not ceased to kiss My feet. "You did not anoint My head with oil, but she anointed My feet with perfume. "For this reason I say to you, her sins, which are many, have been forgiven, for she loved much; but he who is forgiven little, loves little." And He said to her, "Your sins have been forgiven." And those who were reclining at the table with Him began to say to themselves, "Who is this man who even forgives sins?" And He said to the woman, "Your faith has saved you; go in peace."
(Luke 7:34-50).

Throughout the life of Jesus there are many occasions where He interacts with those who were frowned upon by the more cultured people of society. Such actions on the part of Jesus did not put Him in good standing with many of the proper religious people of His day, and yet, He was constantly spending time with these commoners to the detriment of His own reputation. Why? One explanation is that Jesus was more concerned with following the will of the Father than He was with His own reputation. I wonder if the same can be said of us. Have we become so concerned with being the leader that we have forgotten to follow the Lord and be more concerned with His reputation among men than our own?

Please understand, through the use of these examples, I am not advocating anything other than an examination and re-evaluation of how the life of Jesus is presented as support for some current leadership principles. I do believe we must include the whole of Jesus' life in our understanding of how He led others and that Jesus' primary concern was to follow the will of the Father.

By now you have come to realize that my perspective on leaders in the Bible is substantively different from much of the leadership literature. One person with whom I have a particular problem considering as a leader is Moses. Yet, he is probably the most cited person in the Old Testament about whom we are told we can learn how to lead others. My contention is that Moses was not a leader, but a follower. Consider the following:

1. **Moses was told what to do (Exodus 3:10).**
2. **Moses was told what to say (Exodus 3:12-18).**
3. **Moses was told what would happen (Exodus 3:19-22).**
4. **Moses followed the cloud by day and the pillar of fire by night (Exodus 13:21).**

Throughout the story of the Exodus we read where, "Moses and Aaron did just as the LORD commanded them" (Exodus 7:6). Psalms 77: 20 records the most accurate portrayal of the work of Moses by declaring to God, "You led your people like a flock, by the hand of Moses and Aaron." God was doing the leading. Moses was God's "hand." In fact, the only times Moses acted as a leader were when he got angry and broke the initial set of tablets at the sight of the golden calf (Exodus 32:19) and when he struck the rock twice (Number 20:11-12), an event that cost him his entrance into the promised land. Some may argue that Moses was acting as a leader when, in order to keep his sanity, he took the advice of his father-in-law to divide the people into more manageable groups and set judges over these groups (Exodus 18:13-26). I would argue that this was not so much leadership as management. This action did not give the people a new vision or lead the people in a new direction. It merely allowed for more efficient caring for the people as they followed the direction of the Lord. In reality, Moses exemplifies the type of follower needed in today's church: one who understands the Word of God and seeks to fulfill it regardless of their position within the organization.

The best reason I can think of as to why these events in the life of Moses and these unique leadership events in the life of Jesus are not mentioned in our leadership texts is because these events do not fit the template of what much of the literature portrays leadership to be. However, if we allow the leadership literature to determine what we teach from the Bible, then we must ask ourselves, "Are we teaching what the Bible says, or are we simply proof-texting what we *want* the Bible to say and teaching this as biblical truth?"

From a follower perspective it is clear that all of Jesus' actions have their genesis in a desire to fulfill the will of the Father. His overwhelming desire to honor His Father and fulfill His purpose on earth was the reason why Jesus' actions were sometimes conventional and sometimes unique. As followers of Christ, we must interpret Jesus' actions and words from the same perspective He had, the perspective of a follower.

Anti-Follower Bias

I distinctly remember having a conversation with a man several years ago that started badly and rapidly deteriorated into a full-blown confrontation. It seemed that every attempt I made to engage the man in a civil conversation was met with heated resistance. I finally abandoned my efforts at friendship and retreated to the safety of my home and the confidential ear of my wife. As I shared with her my experience, she asked one question that clarified much of what I had experienced. She asked, "Did you tell him you were a pastor?" When I shared with her that I began the conversation by telling him I was a pastor, she informed me that the man had a history of bad experiences with pastors and did not want anything to do with them. With that new piece of information I realized that this man's resistance to my overtures of friendship was not personal in as much as it was the result of an ingrained bias against pastors.

We all have our biases. I am biased against my college Alma Mater's football opponents. I am biased against anchovies. I am biased

47

for followers. Bias is a predisposition either favorably or negatively toward an object or a person usually based upon some past experience. It may be that past experiences with some poorly behaving followers have led to a generalized bias within leadership literature against followers. It may be that some followers have developed a bias against leaders because of some authoritative, over-bearing leaders with whom they have had to deal with in the past. We all have our biases.

However, it wasn't until I began to try and understand life and organizations from a follower perspective that I noticed the overt negative bias toward followers in the leadership literature. Many leadership writers concede that everyone is a follower on some level, but the implication is that being a follower is secondary to becoming a leader. Other writers will imply that following is not a priority, much less a privileged position with important responsibilities. The following are just a few excerpts from one writer:

- "Followers tell you what you want to hear. Leaders tell you what you need to hear".[6]

- "Any leader who has only followers around him will be called upon to continually draw on his own resources to get things done."[7]

- "Followers will always weigh the advantage/disadvantage issue in light of personal gain/loss, not organizational gain/loss."[8]

- "Followers need leaders able to effectively navigate for them."[9]

- "The bottom line for followers is what a leader is capable of."[10]

- "Followers simply cannot develop leaders."[11]

I am certain that this particular author did not intend for his comments to be perceived as being anti-follower. However, from these comments it is painfully obvious that the author has a bias against being a follower. But then, this particular author is not alone in his opinion. Leadership books consistently proclaim that it takes leaders to make a difference. Leaders are special. The constant message from the culture is a person needs to aspire to be the leader. Businesses don't spend thousands of dollars teaching employees how to aspire to become followers (although in my opinion they should). Parents do not stand on the sideline of the soccer game and encourage their young player to, "Get in there and be a real follower." Such thinking is not largely accepted in our independently minded, western American culture. Being the leader is the prize position. The leader takes the spotlight in business and the church.

Please understand. I believe the Bible clearly teaches that leaders are a necessary part of any organization, especially the church (Hebrews 13: 7, 17, 24). An emphasis on followers is not a de-emphasis on leaders. It is merely a re-examination of the role and responsibilities of followers and leaders within the unique organizational culture of a church. Every organization has a culture, and I explain some aspects of this in Chapter 8. However, my position is that church organizational culture is different (by divine design I might add) than any other organization on the planet. This uniqueness may be why many within the church refer to the church as an organism, a living entity operating through the power of the Holy Spirit. However we perceive the church, its organizational culture does not revolve around position and rank (power and control) but service and responsibility (obedience). A Follower First philosophy emphasizes this role and responsibility for every follower of Christ.

Short Circuiting the Process

In our zeal to have the church make an impact on the world we have begun teaching about leadership and training leaders without first fully embracing the process by which leaders are established in the church. This lack of understanding short-circuits the church's impact and effectiveness in the world. Although we certainly need leaders and leader training, the emphasis within all Christian organizations needs to be that before we accept the role of leader, we recognize that we are Followers First. I do not subscribe to the theory that to be a good leader you first need to learn to be a good follower. Many times when people make this statement they imply that being a follower is a stepping stone toward the ultimate prize of becoming the leader. This is NOT what I am proposing. I propose:

GOOD LEADERS ARE GOOD FOLLOWERS.

When we take on the responsibility of being leaders, we don't quit being followers. Christian leaders in all organizations must begin to think of themselves as Followers First. Consider Figure 1 and the process by which a follower of Christ assumes a leader role.

Figure 1: A Leader is Born

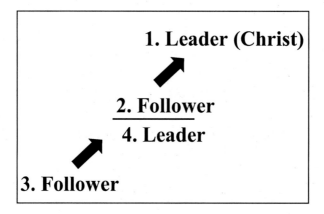

In the first position is Christ Jesus. Because of the work He has done in our hearts and because He is the Head of the Church, we all follow Him. Christ's position puts all believers in the second position as followers. This relational position is primary in all our affairs. However, over time we may be asked to serve in positions of responsibility over other persons within the church organization. Such a role would mean that we would have followers in position number three. The people in position number three, then, would naturally refer to those in position number two as their leader, position number four. In the church, the primary responsibility of those in leader position number four is, as a fellow follower, to lead the followers in position three to follow Jesus.

A subtle temptation occurs, however, when the followers in position two begin to believe what the followers in position three call them (leaders) more than believing what the One in position one (Christ) calls them because Christ calls them who they really are, followers. In the church, if a leader begins to act in the role of a leader without understanding that he or she is responsible for being a follower first, that leader runs the risk of leading in ways that may not honor the One whom they profess to follow. In the church, if someone seeks to become a leader without first being a committed follower, that person can do grave damage to the relationships within the Body of Christ. Paul may be alluding to this understanding of who you really are in Christ when he tells Timothy not to appoint new believers too quickly to leader positions (1 Timothy 3:5).

By teaching leadership alone, with little to no regard for what it means to be a follower, we are training people to lead without understanding their primary purpose for being a part of the church in the first place: to follow Christ. We teach leaders how to accomplish goals and tasks through people without understanding the primary goal and task of every endeavor is to know God through the person of Jesus Christ and introduce others to Him. Perhaps this is why so often our building projects, special events, and daily routines become endurance exercises rather than opportunities to experience the presence of the Lord. Perhaps the growing number of church splits, conflicts, and ministerial dismissals are the result of our current crop of leaders assuming responsibilities, as taught by the business models, they have no business assuming within a church organizational culture. Perhaps current leadership teaching places responsibilities on church leaders that the Bible does not suggest (i.e. everything rises or falls on leadership). Perhaps it is time for leaders and followers to return to a different position, the position of humility and submission, the position of being a Follower First.

What Might Happen?

What would happen if the church embraced a Follower First philosophy? What if everyone in the church saw himself or herself as a follower: pastors, pre-school workers, teachers and parking attendants?

What if church members recognized the difference between each group as one of responsibility, not of position or worth or calling? With a follower first philosophy, the pastor understands himself to be a follower of Christ whose responsibility is to shepherd the flock of God:

> The elders who are among you I exhort, I who am a fellow elder and a witness of the sufferings of Christ, and also a partaker of the glory that will be revealed: Shepherd the flock of God which is among you, serving as overseers, not by compulsion but willingly, not for dishonest gain but eagerly; nor as being lords over those entrusted to you, but being examples to the flock; and when the Chief Shepherd appears, you will receive the crown of glory that does not fade away (1 Peter 5:2).

With a Follower First philosophy, pastors understand they have a responsibility to shepherd the flock as they have been told by the Owner of the flock [Jesus owns His flock (1 Corinthians 6:20; 7:23) and is the Lord of the church.] Likewise, pre-school workers see themselves as followers of Christ whose responsibility is to nurture the youngest babies and toddlers for of such is the kingdom of heaven. Bible teachers understand they are followers of Christ with the responsibility to teach accurately the Word of God. Parking attendants see themselves as being followers of Christ with the responsibility of making certain those who attend find a place to park and are greeted warmly. Gone are the yearnings over rank and title and hierarchy. Titles are understood as designating responsibility before God. A Follower First philosophy understands the beauty and power of submission. A Follower First philosophy trusts in the work of the Holy Spirit and rests in the sovereignty of a living God to protect His Bride. A Follower First philosophy confronts the pew-sitter mentality of many who may simply be attending church for the show.

With a Follower First philosophy, excuses about not fully participating in the church are eliminated. If church members are truly followers of Christ, they have a responsibility to obey (follow) Him. Further, they have a responsibility to discover and then fulfill their important place in the Body of Christ, His church. Just because a church member does not have the title leader ascribed to their responsibility does not make their work any less important in God's plan than those who hold titular positions of responsibility. Within a Follower First philosophy Christians don't have to wait to be a leader to make an impact and be influential in the lives of others. As a follower of Christ, influence is a given.

Conclusion

I hope these few chapters will encourage the church to question some of these preconceived ideas about leading and discover the simple truth that the church of Jesus Christ actually operates best with a Follower First philosophy. I realize that the idea of being a follower is often denigrated as a position with little to no influence and unworthy of respect. As one student recently commented, "If we implement this philosophy in our churches it will change the way we have pretty much always thought about how the church operates." I agree. However, if we can implement a Follower First philosophy within the church, I believe a genuine revival of obedience on the part of those who have been inactive for years will result. We will see members giving more, participating more, sharing their faith more, and exemplifying the life of Christ more if we raise the level of our understanding regarding what it means to be a follower of Christ. If Christians begin to understand that pastors are humble followers of Christ (just like they are) who is trying to follow the commands of Christ (just like they are), perhaps everyday believers who have never considered themselves spiritual leaders will begin to understand that they don't have to be leaders in order to be influential, spiritual, faithful, followers of Christ. Perhaps if we can instill in followers the idea that faithfully following the Lord is a worthy occupation, that being a follower is a privilege, and that calling ourselves followers carries with it special responsibilities, we will begin to see individuals whom we would never have dreamed become obedient to the commands of Christ.

As you read, embrace who you are as a Follower First. Don't succumb to the fear of not becoming the leader that many teach as the ultimate goal of life. Be the person God has created you to be and then act according to His best interest in the positions of responsibility He gives. In so doing, you will be following the example of the ultimate follower, our Lord Jesus Christ.

Life from a Follower's Perspective

Unintended Consequences
- Church Ineffectiveness
- Church Non-Participation
- Church Division
- Cavalier Interpretations

Anti-Follower Bias

Short Circuiting the Process
- Good leaders ARE good followers.
- A Leader is Born

1. Leader (Christ)

2. Follower
4. Leader

3. Follower

Part II

Embrace Your

Follower Identity

Chapter 3

Followers:
The Overlooked Treasure

I asked several of my colleagues during a roundtable discussion to try and ascertain which type of leadership theory might fit the following five characteristics. The first characteristic was the willingness to assume responsibility. The answers included Transformational Leadership and Transactional Leadership. The second characteristic was the willingness to serve. Most suggested Servant Leadership as the best fit. The third characteristic was the willingness to challenge the status quo and ask questions. Transformational Leadership was the primary answer. The fourth characteristic was the willingness to participate in transformation. Not unexpectedly, Transformational Leadership was again the most mentioned. The fifth characteristic was the willingness to take moral action, such as quitting a job, if the values of the organization were no longer congruent with personal values. Transformational Leaders, Transactional Leaders, and Leader Member Exchange Theory were considerations. (Each of these theories will be discussed later.)

The group was surprised when I disclosed that the five characteristics I had named were not characteristics of leaders but characteristics of Courageous Followers as outlined by Ira Chaleff.[1] Perhaps you are surprised as well to read followers described as having initiative, assuming responsibility, and being willing to challenge leaders. This is not the stereotypical follower that much of the leadership literature describes. In fact, as one ministerial colleague confided, "We need leaders with these characteristics."

As I mentioned previously, the greatest impetus to the inactivity of the church and hindrance to participation in the church is the thinking of those who are members of the church. The time has come to uncover the hidden treasure of followers in the church by gaining a new, biblical, and accurate understanding of biblical followers.

Follower Misconceptions

The misconceptions of followers developed over time in the leadership literature often hinder an accurate understanding of biblical followers. The following examples represent a sampling of such misconceptions.

Sheepness

Perhaps the greatest misconception of followers is exacerbated by the use of the term *sheep.* The New Testament uses this word metaphorically to identify those persons who have believed upon the Lord Jesus Christ and belong to the Father as well as to those who wander "as sheep without a shepherd" (Matthew 9:36). Throughout the Bible, references are made to the Lord being our Shepherd (Psalm 23) and Jesus referring to believers as, "My sheep" (John 10:27). Such metaphors have given rise to books on how people's actions in the church really do resemble the actions of sheep in many ways. These ways may include not having direction, not being able to care for themselves, or even having the inherent need for someone to lead them.

The only problem with such a perspective is that believers in Christ are *not* sheep. They are human beings. Granted, some may be fearful. Some may lose their way, but not all. The idea of the people in the church **being** sheep is often joked about among ministers. While teaching my classes, occasionally a pastor may mention he is frustrated because the church people will not change or that many within the congregation continue to make poor decisions. It is not uncommon for someone to jokingly assert, "What do you expect; they're sheep!" followed by confirming laughter. However, I am quick to point out to these students that by consoling ourselves with these assertions, we are forgetting one key truth. Pastors are sheep too.

Such conversations indicate how easily vocational ministers can sometimes begin to think of themselves as better than church members because of their call from God to serve the church. Every vocational minister faces this temptation at some point in ministry. Ministers begin to think that while they may be sheep, they are enlightened sheep. Putting it bluntly, it is as if these ministers are saying, "I may be dumb, but I'm not as dumb as my people." Even worse, what really may be developing is a type of pastoral arrogance in which a call to vocational ministry is accompanied by the belief that the minister is impervious to *sheepness*. It is as if spiritual evolution (if there were such a thing) has made the minister a better sheep than others. If these ideas are left unchecked and ministers carry such ideas forward in working with church people, vocational ministers stand in danger of creating a type of leader aristocracy from which the leaders look down at the followers and show them pity and care for them but never exert the time or energy to equip followers for service. Leaders should be aware that such a condescending attitude is not overlooked by the followers in the church.

Pastors and ministry leaders are often perceived as being better Christians than other people in the church. However, when leaders identify themselves as followers, they can embrace their own *sheepness* and dependency on the leadership of the Great Shepherd. The vocational ministers and leaders need to let the congregation know that all followers of Christ are sheep, but all true followers do not have the negative attributes of sheep. True followers of Christ have the attributes of redeemed humanity and through the process of sanctification are working through their humanness toward completeness in Christ. Pastors and/or elders are those in the church called to help all Jesus' sheep grow toward greater Christ-likeness. The follower-centric organization evidences what the apostle Paul admonishes all followers of Christ to do in Philippians 2:3-4:

> Let nothing be done through selfish ambition or conceit, but in lowliness of mind let each esteem others better than himself.

Nothing in the church is to be done through selfish ambition or conceit. We can have ambition, but it must not be an ambition solely fixed on personal fulfillment. Such a fixation makes the minister conceited. Instead, the minister's ambition should be to make Christ great and show respect to everyone.

Ultimately, the key idea behind the biblical use of the word sheep to describe people is the concept of total dependence. Followers of Christ, His sheep, are to be totally dependent upon Him. The pastor's primary job is not to improve a person's self-concept, but rather, through preaching, teaching, and modeling bring the believer from self-sufficiency to Christ-sufficiency, a state of total dependence upon the Lord Jesus Christ.

Subordinates

A second misconception is to consider fellow followers as subordinates. In the business community the idea of subordinates is usually used for those in the organization who are under the direct supervision of others in the organizational chart. In the military, a subordinate is one who is lower in rank than a superior officer. Though church organizational charts sometime reflect a top-down organizational structure similar to those of businesses and the military, in the follower-leader relationship, these charts function to outline responsibility, not rank. Within the church there is only one superior-subordinate relationship. Jesus is the superior, and all other believers are subordinate. All other working relationships within the Body of Christ are based upon a willing submission toward one another.

Figure 2: Biblical Subordination

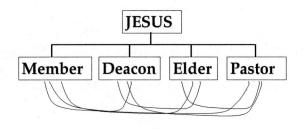

Willing Submission

The organizational diagram above (See Figure 2) illustrates how the Bible understands the concept of subordination. Note that Jesus is *the* Head over all within the church. Every person, whether member, deacon, elder, or pastor is subordinate to His rule over the church. Also note that there are distinctions and divisions of responsibility within the church. Each group has a distinct biblical outline of responsibilities before the Lord and each other. These responsibilities are not carried out through a hierarchy of power and control but rather through a delicate web of mutual submission for each other under the authority of Jesus in obedience to the Word of God. The church does not function in a way that honors God if the members of that church are not willingly submitting themselves to Jesus first and then to those in positions of responsibility within the church. We will explore this concept further in Chapter 5.

Jesus emphasized the incompatibility of power and control through subordination with the willing submission of followers of Christ by comparing those who lead in the world with those who lead God's people. Jesus stated in Mark 10:42-45:

> But Jesus called them to him, and saith unto them, "Ye know that they which are accounted to rule over the Gentiles exercise lordship over them; and their great ones exercise authority upon them. But so shall it not be among you: but whosoever will be great among you, shall be your minister: And whosoever of you

will be the chiefest, shall be servant of all. For even the Son of man came not to be ministered unto, but to minister, and to give his life a ransom for many."

It is clear from this teaching that Jesus intended His followers to understand that they are to lead as those under authority. The head of the church, Jesus, has the authority and all under Him are subject to Him. Because Jesus came as a servant (Matthew 20:28), He chose to set an example for us as One who serves, not as one who needs to be served. As one commentator aptly wrote:

> Gentile rulers... lord it over them, dominating and oppressing their subjects, and exercise authority over them, exploiting them. But it is not to be this way with Jesus' followers who are under God's rule. Whoever aspires to become great among you, let him be your (plural) house servant (<u>diakonos</u>), one who voluntarily renders useful service to others. Whoever aspires to be first (lit., "first among you") let him be a slave (<u>doulos</u>), one who forfeits his own rights in order to serve any and all (cf. comments on <u>Mark 9:35-37</u>). A disciple is to serve others, not his own interests, voluntarily and sacrificially.[2]

Jesus is clearly teaching those who would lead the church to have the disposition and behavior of a servant. Being a servant is one manifestation of what it means to be a follower. Servants perform the duties they are commanded to do. They follow what their authority tells them to do. If we are servants of the Lord Jesus Christ, then we are to have the disposition and behavior of a servant, a follower. Such an attitude is evidenced by a genuine humility (See Philippians 2:8).

Non-functional

A third misconception within the church is that the term follower is viewed as a devotional concept rather than a functional role. As stated previously, when we talk of followers in the church, most assume we are talking about some aspect of discipleship. I concede that the idea of following may appear to be similar to disciple making. However, upon closer inspection, one can see that the term follower refers to both the condition and the role of every born-again person in the church. The idea of being a follower is a state of mind that each church member must grasp and a role that each church member is responsible to fulfill. Because we have not investigated the functional role and responsibilities of followers in the church, the vast majority of followers are left to figure out for themselves what role they perform and how to respond to certain situations. Without a biblical understanding of their role and responsibility, the born-again follower only has business models and worldly philosophies from which to respond. This results in schisms and conflicts as the Spirit wars against the flesh within the organization. Other followers simply choose the role of spectator and sit on the sideline letting others do the work, an unacceptable and non-biblical follower role as well.

I hope to clarify for leaders and followers what these specific roles are and how the two roles function within the Body of Christ. The follower-leader relationship requires an understanding that the training of followers is an absolute priority in the church. Training will be performed by followers who have that specific (leader) responsibility and the training will be received by followers who have the specific (follower) responsibility of being trained. This may sound a bit convoluted, but hopefully the concept will become clearer.

Follower Characteristics

Because the church has been so preoccupied with developing leaders, we have neglected to investigate the functional characteristics of biblical followers. Preoccupation with leaders has led to a paucity of material from a biblical perspective on the characteristics of biblical followers and their role within the church. In this chapter, I offer a cursory introduction to three of the most often cited authors who have investigated the role of followers within organizations. As you read the various characteristics, I offer some biblical support for how these types of followers respond within the context of a church organization. Hopefully this understanding will give us a preliminary guideline for understanding the biblical role of followers within the church.

Courageous Followers

Ira Chaleff, author of *Courageous Followership*, identified five characteristics of courageous followers. Table 1 outlines the key ideas within each characteristic:

Table 1: Chaleff's Dimensions of Courageous Followership

Dimensions	Description
Assume Responsibility	Courageous followers assume responsibility for themselves and the organization. They do not hold a paternalistic image of the leader or organization. They do not expect the leader or organization to provide for their security and growth or to give them permission to act. Courageous followers discover or create opportunities to fulfill their potential and maximize their value to the organization. They initiate values-based action to improve the organization's external activities and its internal processes. The authority to initiate comes from the courageous follower's understanding and ownership of the common purpose and from the needs of those the organization serves.
Serve	Courageous followers are not afraid of the hard work required to serve a leader. They assume new or additional responsibilities to unburden the leader and serve the organization. They stay alert for areas in which their strengths complement the leader's and assert themselves in these areas. Courageous followers stand up for their leader and the tough decisions a leader must make if the organization is to achieve its purpose. They are as passionate as the leader in pursuing the common purpose.

Dimensions	Description
Challenge	Courageous followers give voice to the discomfort they feel when the behaviors or policies of the leader or group conflict with their sense of what is right. They are willing to stand up, stand out, risk rejection, and initiate conflict in order to examine the actions of the leader and group when appropriate. They are willing to deal with the emotions their challenge evokes in the leader and group. Courageous followers value organizational harmony and their relationship with the leader, but not at the expense of the common purpose and their integrity.
Participate in Transformation	When behavior that jeopardizes the common purpose remains unchanged, courageous followers recognize the need for transformation. They champion the need for change and stay with the leader and group while they mutually struggle with the difficulty of real change. They examine their own need for transformation and become full participants in the change process as appropriate.
Take Moral Action	Courageous followers know when it is time to take a stand that is different than that of the leaders. They are answering to a higher set of values. The stand may involve refusing to obey a direct order, appealing the order to the next level of authority, or tendering one's resignation. These and other forms of moral action involve personal risk. But, service to the common purpose justifies and sometimes demands acting.

Looking at the follower characteristics in Table 1, do Courageous Followers who are believers have a place in our churches? If so, how should we integrate Courageous Followers into the life of the church, and how should these Courageous Followers operate as biblical followers? I offer the following ideas for discussion.

Assume Responsibility

As a biblical follower, each of us has a responsibility. As followers of Christ, it is our responsibility to see that the church fulfills the Great Commission. It is NOT the responsibility of leaders to motivate us out of our mediocrity (as if they could). If we are complacent and mediocre in our service in the church, it is a reflection of our mediocre love for Jesus and/or our lack of understanding our responsibilities before God, not the pastor's inability to lead us. The pastor or elders of the church are not our parents. They may care for us and watch over us, but we are not babies. We are followers of Christ, and as such, we will learn how to feed ourselves, clothe ourselves, and help others do the same. If our leaders are not fulfilling the commands of Christ, this does not give us the right to sit around and do nothing but complain and gossip about how we would do things differently. Our responsibility is to obey Christ. If the leaders don't share the gospel or invite people to church to hear the Word, then we will. If the leaders don't teach people the Word of God, we will learn it and teach it. If the church needs input on how to solve problems, we will give it respectfully and submissively. If our assessment of our church is that it is not doing what it ought to do, **we will not blame the leader(s); we will blame ourselves.** We are followers of Christ. We willingly assume our God-given responsibility.

Serve

God gives the church leaders. If we believe God placed these leaders in their roles of responsibility, we should be committed to serve alongside them and to serve them. In Hebrews 13:17 the writer commands that we submit to those who "rule" over us. As such, we are to let these persons perceive us as a brothers and sisters in Christ, fellow followers who can be trusted to be on the team. We will add our

66

strengths to our leaders' weaknesses without making them feel the lesser or giving ourselves any credit. As followers, we are servants of Christ (John 12:26). As such, our joy is to serve the servants of Christ. Jesus said, "If anyone serves Me, let him follow Me; and where I am, there My servant will be also" (John 12:26). **Followers want to be where Christ is being served.** We will not be a burden to our leaders but will find where we are needed in the organization without waiting to be asked. (Requiring that someone ask me to do ministry in the church often reflects a veiled, pride-filled attitude that becomes an excuse for my own inactivity.) We will stand up for our leaders and stand with our leaders as long as they are following our Leader, the Lord Jesus Christ. By doing so, it will be profitable for us as our leaders are allowed to minister with "joy and not with grief" (Hebrews 13:17b).

Challenge

As followers of Christ we realize our frailties and that the leaders whom God has placed in our lives are human as well. Therefore, we will not expect perfection from them. We will not make our expectations more than the Bible requires. If, however, the leaders move in a direction that directly contradicts the clear teaching of the Bible or lead in such a way that the reputation of Christ might be besmirched, then it is our duty as followers of Christ first, to speak directly to the leader(s). We will not speak to our little group and form an army of sympathizers before challenging the leader(s). This would be gossip and murmuring, and we will have no part in allowing the devil to use us and this verbal mechanism to bring discord and division to the Body of Christ. Instead, each follower should contact the leader and speak respectfully, lovingly, and caringly, in a Spirit-filled manner to point out where there is a potential problem. Like the prophet Nathan with King David (2 Samuel 12:7), each follower should be ready to risk the death of a personal relationship in order to respond biblically and follow the commands of Christ. Followers must be willing to allow the leader(s) to misunderstand them and receive the likely negative emotional response from the leaders at such a challenge. Regardless of the response, followers should seek the unity of the Spirit in the bond of peace (Ephesians 4:3) at all times, never willing to compromise the Word of God or the reputation of *the* Leader, the Lord Jesus Christ, for personal gain.

Participate in Transformation

As followers of Christ we realize that negotiating change within an organization is one of the most time consuming and upsetting events in the life of any organization. We will embrace change and encourage those around us to do the same. We will share our insights on what actions can best be taken to help the congregation through the change process, and then we will make ourselves available to enact the needed change. We will focus on the future of what will be rather than look back at the past loss of what was. We will change internally, spiritually, and emotionally. We will not gripe and complain at the changes that have affected us. As the mercies of God are new every morning (Lamentations 3:23), we will have a new and refreshing attitude of seeking to know God and be changed by Him through every context of the day, especially when operating within the church.

Take Moral Action

Followers support God-called leaders in the church. However, if the time comes when we can no longer follow their leading because of immorality or straying from following the Lord by not following the Word of God, we have the moral obligation to challenge the leader and lovingly direct him to the Word and correction according to Matthew 18. However, if the leader continues to dishonor God, followers of Christ have a moral obligation to leave the organization rather than cause a split within the Body. If leaving is the last resort, followers should do so quietly and without fanfare. When friends ask why we are leaving, give them a substantive, biblical (not personal) reason and no more. Followers should not brag, gossip, murmur, or gather "prayer groups" together to pray for the pastor's repentance. Followers do not lead rebellions nor do they play the martyr. Once the decision is made to leave, they follow Christ to another church and submit to the leader(s) of that Body of Christ to the glory of God.

Exemplary Followers

Before Chaleff introduced the courageous follower concept, Robert Kelley proposed we look for exemplary followers. Kelley's book, *The Power of Followership*[3], provides further insights into the world of effective followers and how important they are to an organization. In 1988, Kelley wrote an article for the Harvard Business Review in which he stated, "Followership is not a person but a role, and what distinguishes followers from leaders is not intelligence or character but the role they play."[4] Kelley further stated, "What distinguishes an effective follower from an ineffective follower is enthusiastic, intelligent, and self-reliant participation—without star billing—in the pursuit of an organizational goal."[5] Kelley attributed four qualities to the effective follower: (a) self-management, (b) commitment, (c) competence and focus, and (d) courage (See Table 2).

Table 2: Kelley's Dimensions of Effective Followers

Dimensions	Explanation
Self-management	The key to being an effective follower is the ability to think for one-self, to exercise control and independence and to work without close supervision. Good followers are people to whom a leader can safely delegate responsibility, people who anticipate needs at their own level of competence and authority.
Commitment	Effective followers are committed to something—a cause, a product, an organization, an idea—in addition to the care of their own lives and careers.

69

Competence and focus	Effective followers master skills that will be useful to their organizations. They generally hold higher performance standards than the work environment requires and continuing education is second nature to them. It is a staple in their professional development.
Courage	Effective followers are credible, honest, and courageous. They establish themselves as independent, critical thinkers whose knowledge and judgment can be trusted. They give credit where credit is due, admitting mistakes and sharing successes. They form their own views and ethical standards and stand up for what they believe.

Self-management

To the biblical follower, self-management, as well as self-discipline, is focused not so much on self as on Christ. The follower's dependence upon the person of the Holy Spirit for the enabling necessary to fulfill the commands of Christ is essential to bringing glory to God. Within the context of the Holy Spirit's leading, each biblical follower is his or her own person. Biblical followers have gifts and abilities that can be used in the fulfillment of the work of the Lord within the church (Consider Romans 12:6; 1Corinthians 4-11). A spirit-filled follower knows and exercises spiritual discipline and does not need close supervision once a task has been assigned. The biblical follower works through difficulties without the leader's intervention (thus freeing the leader), and is able to gather other followers to participate in the fulfillment of the responsibility.

Commitment

The biblical follower's commitment is not to a cause or an organization but to a person, the Lord Jesus Christ. This is one of the distinguishing characteristics of the Following-Leader we will discuss in

70

Chapter Six. Because the follower is committed to Christ, he/she will be committed to what Christ is committed. Jesus is committed to the Father. Thus, the follower's focus for each day is the glory of God the Father. Jesus is committed to His church. Thus, all true followers of Christ will be committed to His church, not just universally but locally. Personal ambitions, careers, and advancements take a back seat to the person of Christ and the commands He gives to "love the Lord your God with all your heart, and with all your soul, and with all your mind" (Matthew 22:37-38).

Competence and Focus

The biblical follower is a learner, a disciple. Followers are continually seeking to know more of Christ and His Word. They sharpen their skills and take the necessary time, effort, and resources to find excellence in everything they do. They desire to be "approved unto God" (2 Timothy 2:15). Therefore, they study, read, memorize, meditate, and apply the Word to their daily lives. They take advantage of times of development offered by the church and, if none are available, will seek other sources (internet, colleges, etc.) to further their understanding of what it means to honor God through Jesus Christ.

Courage

Ira Chaleff has already decribed this characteristic of a biblical follower. Suffice it to say that the biblical follower is credible. That is, the follower has personal integrity. Their yes is yes, and their no is no (Matthew 5:37). The follower will not talk behind the back of the leader. They speak the truth even at the risk of being misunderstood. Their integrity before the Lord is to love and serve the leader. Loving the leader sometimes means holding the leader accountable and making certain that the leader knows and understands facts, not politically motivated spin. Biblical followers will not succumb to the temptation of self-preservation but will make every effort to see that the Word of God is obeyed at all times.

Post-industrial Followers

Joseph Rost takes a different approach proposing that leadership be considered in light of a post-industrialized culture.[6] Because the Bible was written in a pre-industrialized society, many of Rost's ideas resonate well with Follower First thinking. Focusing on the follower-leader relationship in the historic context in which these relationships occur gives us a new perspective on the reality of the interdependence required within this relationship.

Rost suggests five dynamics of a follower-leader relationship:

Leaders are Followers

> Only people who are active in the leadership process are followers. Passive people are not in a relationship. They have chosen not to be involved. They cannot have influence. Passive people are not followers.[7]

One of the keys to understanding biblical followers is the realization that followers are not stagnant but active. Following is an action. The very meaning of the word requires the follower to actively pursue the Lord Jesus Christ. Within the church, followers are actively engaged in the process of seeking out those who are leaders and presenting themselves for service.

Followers Influence Leaders

> Active people can fall anywhere on a continuum of activity from highly active to minimally active, and their influence in the leadership process is, in large part, based on their activity, their willingness to get involved, their use of the power resources they have at their command to influence other people. Some followers are very active; others are not so active. Some followers are very active at certain times and not so active at other times.[8]

Biblical follower activity is based upon the freedom the followers have to exercise their gifts, talents and abilities. This level of follower activity is based upon two aspects. First, a follower's level of intimacy with the Leader, the Lord Jesus Christ, determines the level and activity of following within the context of the church. Followers who have a keen desire to know Christ in all aspects of life are usually actively engaged in the process of making Christ known resulting in these followers having a greater degree of responsibility and influence in the church and among the leaders. Second, the titular leaders of the church must establish a permission giving atmosphere in which the follower is secure to initiate activity without fear of reprisal. Leaders do not empower followers. Rather leaders create the structural freedom in which followers can exercise their gifts and abilities. Such freedom results in high follower participation and greater productivity.

Follower Reciprocality

> Followers can become leaders and leaders can become followers in any one leadership relationship. People are not stuck in one or the other for the whole time the relationship exits. Followers may be leaders for a while, and leaders may be followers for a while. Followers do not have to be managers to be leaders. This ability to change places without changing organizational positions gives followers considerable influence and mobility.[9]

The interdependent nature and the humility required of persons within the biblical follower-leader relationship allow both followers and leaders the freedom to serve within the scope of their giftedness. In a follower-centric organization, position and rank are not highly prized. Therefore, followers and leaders can cooperate with each other under the lordship of Christ without fear of being replaced or being upstaged by someone else. The end result of honoring God by fulfilling His commands trumps any prideful and arrogant thinking of holding on to a title or position. (See the explanation of the Mobius Strip on page 80.)

Follower Flexibility

> In one group or organization people can be leaders. In other groups and organizations they can be followers. Followers are not always followers in all leadership relationships.[10]

Biblical followers do not see being a leader as better than being a follower. Therefore, the follower is comfortable in whatever position within the organization the providence of the Lord may allow. In one instance the biblical follower may be the titular leader of a business or in a management position within a company. At the same time, this biblical follower may also be a member of a local church. Because of the Follower First mindset, the biblical follower who may be a leader at work can operate within the church without feelings of resentment because he/she is not a titular leader. In fact, biblical followers hold no expectations that their positions at secular jobs give them any greater influence within the church. The thought process of the biblical follower is never to perceive himself or herself as leader, but rather as a follower in a specific position within the organization. The flexibility of the biblical follower allows the person to respond according to need, title or position not withstanding.

Followers Lead

Joseph Rost summarizes the essential nature of a follower-leader relationship by pointing out that *together,* followers and leaders get things accomplished. Together, those in positions of leading and those who are in positions of following lead the organization to accomplish the goals. Rost said:

> Most important, followers do not do followership, they do leadership. Both leaders and followers form one relationship that is leadership. There is no such thing as followership in the new school of leadership. Followership makes sense only in the industrial leadership paradigm, where leadership is good management. . . . Followers and leaders develop a relationship

wherein they influence one another as well as the organization and society, and that is leadership. They do not do the same things in the relationship, just as composers and musicians do not do the same thing in making music, but they are both essential to leadership.[11]

Within the follower-centric organization, followers are not viewed as mere necessities in order to accomplish goals, but to use Rost's words, followers are "essential" in the process of leading the church to fulfill her mission. Followers influence others and have an impact on everyone around them. Biblical followers are aware of this awesome responsibility and guard how they respond because the glory of their Leader, the Lord Jesus, is always at stake.

Dishonoring Follower Types

We have spent most of our time examining positive follower types and how they might be evidenced in a church context. Yet there are some who call themselves followers who do not manifest the characteristics of those who embrace the Follower First philosophy. Unfortunately, these pseudo-followers are the people who discourage leaders and give faithful followers a bad reputation. The following are a few dishonoring follower types who sometime appear within the church.

Angry Followers

Angry followers have become hurt or angry because of a breach of trust or unmet expectations. These followers have violated one of the key rules of being a biblical follower. They have allowed a breach of trust or unmet expectations to form a division between them and the leader. They have not pursued the leader and gotten a definitive answer to the situation. They may have relied upon speculation and even third-party gossip to form unfounded opinions about the leader. These followers need to confess their sin to God, repent, and humble

75

themselves to the leader. They especially need to make right any wrongs (character assassinations) done to the leader through sharing gossip or innuendo with others. If after these actions have been corrected and the follower and leader have not been reconciled, other church leaders may need to intervene at the request of the leader and follower in order to clarify the situation and make any corrections that might facilitate reconciliation according to Mathew 18. Angry alienated followers are not biblical followers. They are cysts within the Body of Christ and can often become cancerous, spreading their poisonous attitudes and infecting others.

Whatever Followers

Whatever followers lose credibility because they do not think for themselves. By not thinking for themselves, these whatever followers are not being circumspect in their daily lives. They are not good stewards of their minds. They may have poor self-concepts which evidence a lack of understanding of who they are in Christ. Additionally, these whatever followers usually want everyone to simply get along. Peace at any price is their mantra, whether it is peace at the expense of truth or not. They are not actively engaged and connected with the person of Christ, are not walking in the power of the Holy Spirit, and leave themselves open to being led astray by those who distort biblical teaching (2 Timothy 3:6).

Mediocre Followers

Mediocre followers perform required tasks minimally and look out for themselves. They follow the adage that the one rule of the army is never to volunteer for anything. Thus, they never volunteer or offer themselves for service other than that which is the minimum necessary to maintain status in the group. They are proficient in the politics of church, knowing how to be for and against a particular issue at any given time. They make it a point not to cross powerful people and to be on the winning side of a discussion. In the church, these followers will come, sit, give their five dollars a week, carry their Bible, sing the songs, and smile with everyone else. They will, however, not honor God by giving their lives in service to Christ. They do not experience the joy of second-mile service (Matthew 5:41). Their desire is to never be challenged or personally extended to the point of relying solely upon the work of the Holy Spirit to get a job done. Their lives are mediocre. The bread of life to them is stale and tasteless.

Maintenance Followers

Maintenance followers lack initiative, require constant direction, and look to leaders to do their thinking. They represent the stereotypical *sheep* that so many believe make up the church. These people do not honor the Lord with their lives and fall short of the Lord's command to deny self, take up their cross daily and follow Jesus. However, what is striking about these followers is that their attitudes and actions may be exacerbated by the leader-centered philosophy in the church. When the people are taught that the leaders have the vision, the goals, and the gifts to do the work of the Lord, why should followers think about such things? If all the leaders want is for followers to fulfill the leader's vision, could this be a reason for a lack of initiative? Because these followers have not engaged or perhaps haven't even been consulted regarding their vision, goals, and desires, there is no buy-in to the direction of the church and certainly no participation. These followers have been brainwashed into believing that they are not a vital part of the body and, as a result, become inactive and despondent. They are fully convinced that they are nobodies in the great scheme of things.

Conclusion

One of the best symbols I have found regarding the nature of the follower-leader relationship is the Mobius strip (See Figure 3).[12] Taken from topographical mathematics, the unique quality of this geometric shape is that it only has one continuous surface. A twist in the band allows one to traverse the surface of the band without ever crossing a boundary.[13]

Figure 3: Mobius Strip

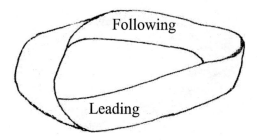

By having only one surface, the Mobius strip is the perfect example of how leading and following take place. A follower may be a leader and a leader a follower in a given context. This is often the case in team meetings in which the leader of the team may be less informed about a matter than another and permits the follower to take the lead in the discussion and decision making. With this view, *leadership becomes a reciprocal, interdependent relationship between a leader and a follower.* Such an understanding of leadership allows for a fluid functioning of the gifts and abilities of positional followers and leaders. It may still fall to the titular leader of the group to make the final decision, but the interplay between the leader and follower usually results in a better decision and more buy-in on the part of the group.

Understanding the leader-follower relationship from this perspective raises the value of followers within an organization. Leading is not a linear activity in which the leader acts and the followers respond. The Mobius strip exemplifies that followers play a much more important role in the process of accomplishing goals and objectives than simply fulfilling the wishes of the leaders. In fact, from the definitions we have investigated, Exemplary and Courageous Followers play an integral part in making leaders successful, developing organizational vision, and accomplishing organizational objectives. This is all the more true within churches.

With a Follower First philosophy, every person within the church is given the responsibility to use his or her gifts to fulfill the commands of Christ. Followers who understand their divine role and operate in the power of the Holy Spirit hold the key to accomplishing the world mission of this God-established organization.

Chaleff, Kelley, and Rost, have influenced much of what we know and understand about followers. There is much work to be done to identify specific organizational traits and behaviors of a follower of Christ. However, **willingly following the Lord Jesus Christ with all one's heart, mind, soul, and strength in every circumstance regardless of organizational position** appears to be a good starting point from which we can further explore the treasures of these unique people who make up our unique church organizations.

<u>Followers: The Overlooked Treasure</u>

Follower Misconceptions
- **Sheepness**
- **Subordinates**
- **Non-functional**

Follower Characteristics
    Courageous Followers – Ira Chaleff
- **Assume Responsibility**
- **Serve**
- **Challenge**
- **Participate in Transformation**
- **Take Moral Action**

    Exemplary Followers – Robert Kelley
- **Self-management**
- **Commitment**
- **Competence and Focus**
- **Courage**

    Dishonoring Follower Types
- **Angry**
- **Whatever**
- **Mediocre**
- **Maintenance**

    Post-Industrial Followers – Joseph Rost
- **Leaders are Followers**
- **Followers Influence Leaders**
- **Follower Reciprocality**
- **Follower Flexibility**
- **Followers Lead**

The Mobius Strip

Chapter 4

Follower Identity:
The Freedom to Be

After studying the material to this point, it is not uncommon for students to make their way to me after class with questioning grins on their faces, and before they can say a word I say, "That's right." They usually reply, "That's right what?" I respond, "I'm answering your question, because you were going to ask me if, as a follower of Christ, all you had to do was to be who God has created you to be. And all I'm saying is that's right. That's all you need to be." At this point they usually smile and let out a, "Whew." This response is typical of those who have tied themselves up in a knot trying to be *the leader* as outlined by much of the current leadership literature. Their experience was the same as mine. In an attempt to be the very best leader they could be for Christ, they had forgotten that their first priority was to be the person God had created them to be, a follower. The grins usually turn to laughter as a mountain of self-imposed expectations rolls off their shoulders. They become free: free to be the person God called them to be and, ironically, a more effective leader.

These students realize that their identity as a Follower First makes learning leader skills and developing leader traits much easier. Placed upon the foundation of a Follower First philosophy, leader principles and practices are no longer burdensome. These principles are understood as a means of developing greater influence in the lives of others so that other followers can know the freedom of being a Follower First. As followers of Christ begin to embrace the idea of being a faithful follower, they begin to develop and embrace an identity which, to a watching world, appears to be extremely paradoxical.

The Follower Paradox

Our God is a God who teaches through paradox. The Scriptures reveal that some of the greatest truths are those that resonate in our minds as paradoxical to our intuitive reasoning. Consider the following examples:

Find Life by Losing It

> Matthew 10:37-39
> He who loves father or mother more than Me is not worthy of Me. And he who loves son or daughter more than Me is not worthy of Me. And he who does not take his cross and follow after Me is not worthy of Me. He who finds his life will lose it, and he who loses his life for My sake will find it.

It is not by coincidence that Jesus' teaching on how to find and lose your life follows three expressions of what it means to be worthy to follow Christ. Note the three relationships mentioned. The first is the parental relationship. Even those who gave you life and cared for you cannot be the primary aim of a follower of Christ. The second relationship is that of a son or daughter. Here again the emphasis is that a follower's relationship with sons and daughters is secondary to one's relationship with Christ. The third relationship is that of a person who holds an accurate self-assessment. The follower of Christ is aware of the areas of life where a denial of self must take place. The cross is where those who have been leading their own lives meet Jesus and submit to His life-giving forgiveness. For the believer, then, the cross becomes the place of death for any personal proclivity that might take precedence over the follower's relationship with Jesus. Far from a focus on death, the cross actually becomes the door through which the believer finds the resurrection power of Jesus. Therefore, if a follower finds his/her life in the person of Jesus Christ, that follower will think nothing of putting that life on the line. He/she will lose it. As a result of losing it for the sake of Christ, the follower is guaranteed that he/she will find true life, a life in relationship with God the Father, Son, and Holy Spirit.

Be Strong by Becoming Weak

> 2 Corinthians 12:7-10
> And lest I should be exalted above measure by the abundance of the revelations, a thorn in the flesh was given to me, a messenger of Satan to buffet me, lest I be exalted above measure. Concerning this thing I pleaded with the Lord three times that it might depart from me. And He said to me, "My grace is sufficient for you, for My strength is made perfect in weakness." Therefore most gladly I will rather boast in my infirmities, that the power of Christ may rest upon me. Therefore I take pleasure in infirmities, in reproaches, in needs, in persecutions, in distresses, for Christ's sake. <u>For when I am weak, then I am strong.</u>

We read much about becoming a strong leader. However, if we are to lead in the power of the Holy Spirit by the grace of the Lord Jesus Christ, it appears we must be weak leaders (i.e. Followers First). It is a vital paradox for us to remember that when we are weak, we are strong. A Christian leader cannot allow his/her self-assessment to dictate what will or will not be attempted, what commands will or will not be obeyed, or what he or she can or cannot accomplish. The work of the Lord is not contingent upon the strength of the leader but rather upon the leader's submission and dependence upon Christ. When the leader is most dependent, the leader is most influential, because then God must act if anything of lasting significance occurs. By correctly assessing infirmities and short coming, leaders assess themselves as Followers First and rely totally upon the enabling power of the Holy Spirit. Followers, who understand their biblical responsibilities, embrace these frailties, pray for the strength to overcome them, and rely upon God to work for His good pleasure through them and in spite of them. This healthy humility precedes God's granting the grace necessary to assume other responsibilities (James 4:6).

Receive by Giving

> Luke 6:37-38
> "Judge not, and you shall not be judged. Condemn not, and you shall not be condemned. Forgive, and you will be forgiven. <u>Give, and it will be given to you</u>: good measure, pressed down, shaken together, and running over will be put into your bosom. For with the same measure that you use, it will be measured back to you.

In rapid succession, Jesus instructs His followers how they are to conduct themselves in relationship with others. To fully understand what Jesus is saying in this passage, the passage needs to be read in context. Jesus' teaching of not judging or condemning but forgiving and giving is shared within the context of loving your enemies. In so many words, Jesus teaches His followers that their actions will be significantly different from those who do not have a relationship with Him. It is our enemies whom we are not to judge or condemn. It is our enemies to whom we are to give, expecting nothing in return. This unreserved trust in the promises of the Lord makes the life of the follower of Christ distinctive. For the follower, there is no place for manipulation, calculation, or reservation, only trust. Giving to our enemies allows us to receive a greater understanding of God's own beneficence toward us who were once "enemies of God" (Romans 5:10).

How do we find life? We lose it.
How do we become strong? We become weak.
How do we receive? We give.
How do we impact the world? We follow.

Is it too strange to consider that within God's divine design the effectiveness of the church may rest with teaching and developing followers who understand and revel in following Jesus rather than focusing on leaders and leading? Is it possible that God has designed the organizational DNA of His church to operate best with follower cultures because leader-centric cultures create mutations within the church DNA that hinder the growth and effectiveness of the church? Should we at least be teaching biblical followers how to act, and how to follow church leaders? Should be we teaching these concepts with as much intensity and commitment as we have for teaching leaders within the church? Such concepts appear to be organizational paradoxes that have the potential of mystifying the business world and showing a world in need of a Savior how different life is with Jesus as the Leader and with His people as Followers First.

Personalize the Concepts

Over the past several years, as I have wrestled with the idea of being a Follower First, I have tried to simplify my identity as a follower in the body of Christ with the following statements regarding who I am and my responsibility before God. These statements are by no means comprehensive. I offer them as a stimulus to your own thinking in order to discover your own special place as a follower of Christ. I encourage you to read them and contextualize them to who you are and where you are in your relationship with Christ.

IDENTITY
**I am a follower of the person and teachings of
Jesus Christ and the Bible.**

TITLE
I have been given the title, Ambassador of Christ.

MINISTRY
I have been given the ministry of reconciliation.

PLACE
I am a member of the body of Christ.

ROLE
I have a role and responsibility within the body of Christ.

INFLUENCE
I always influence others.

IDENTITY
**I am a follower of the person and teachings of Jesus Christ and the
Bible.**

Being a follower implies action. I am a follower, not a sitter, stander, or sleeper. If I follow I must be actively pursuing Christ. This requires me to learn, read, apply, and humble myself before others.

Saying one is a follower of the person of Christ, is different than when some say they are followers of any other historical person (Gandhi, Mohammed, Buddha) because implicit in the phrase "follower of the person" is the understanding that to follow a *person*, the person whom you follow must be alive. If a leader is buried in a grave, he/she is not going anywhere for someone to follow. Christians believe Christ to have been raised from the dead and that He is with them and intimately involved in their lives through the indwelling person of God the Holy

Spirit. Thus, His followers can truthfully say they follow Him as they are directed by the Holy Spirit through obedience to the Word of God.

When I say I am a follower of the teachings of Christ, I acknowledge the authority of the commands of Scripture, both Old and New Testaments, and that they are "God breathed" (2 Timothy 3:16) teachings for all humanity. Followers of Christ have a high view of Scripture. Otherwise, the follower might want to become the leader in deciding what biblical passage is or is not inspired and worthy of accepting. Biblical followers submit themselves to Christ by following His commands, not only the direct commands of Christ, but also the teachings found in the Old and New Testament. Let me be clear. A true follower of Christ is committed to the whole of Scripture.

In John 14:21 Jesus stated that followers declare their love for Him by following His commands:

> He who has My commandments and keeps them, it is he who loves Me. And he who loves Me will be loved by My Father, and I will love him and manifest Myself to him.

In this context it is appropriate to consider following as an act of worship. The root meaning of the word 'worship' is to prostrate oneself on the ground.[1] When we bow before the Lord, submitting to His will, His Word, and even His established leaders (Titus 3:1), the follower of Christ yields to the Lord's leading. In this way, the attitude of the follower is one of continuous worship to the glory of God.

TITLE
I have been given the title, Ambassador of Christ.

> 2 Corinthians 5:20-21
> Now then, we are ambassadors for Christ, as though God were pleading through us: we implore you on Christ's behalf, be reconciled to God. For He made Him who knew no sin to be sin for us, that we might become the righteousness of God in Him.

When we consider the role of ambassador it is obvious that an ambassador is one who represents the authority of another. The ambassador only has the authority to act if the king whom he represents commands him. Ambassadors do not speak for themselves. They only communicate what the king says. Ambassadors usually serve as the representative of the king in a foreign country. It is easy to see the parallel to our being on the planet and away from our citizenship which is in heaven (Philippians 3:20). I sometimes think it would be better if our church members called each other Ambassador rather than brother or sister. There is nothing wrong with such familial greetings. However, if members called each other by their title, ambassador, perhaps it would remind us all of our responsibility to do the work of the King and to follow Him.

MINISTRY
I have been given the ministry of reconciliation.

> 2 Corinthians 5:17-19
> Therefore, if anyone is in Christ, he is a new creation; old things have passed away; behold, all things have become new. Now all things are of God, who has reconciled us to Himself through Jesus Christ, and has given us the ministry of reconciliation, that is, that God was in Christ reconciling the world to Himself, not imputing their trespasses to them, and has committed to us the word of reconciliation.

Followers of Christ are ministers and as such have a specific ministry. In the church we often say that every member is a minister, but our leader-centric organizational cultures prohibit us from actually accepting such a philosophy. In the typical church, only the ordained pastor and staff members are considered true ministers. However, in a follower-centric organizational culture, it is natural for all the followers of Christ to accept the responsibility of being ministers of reconciliation. From a biblical perspective, every person on the platform from the pastor to all other staff, as well as every believer in the pew or chair who works and participates in the church, is a minister responsible for carrying out his/her ministry of reconciliation. What is the ministry of reconciliation? Paul states it plainly, "...that God was in Christ reconciling the world to Himself, not imputing their trespasses to them" (2 Corinthians 5:19). In other words, sharing the gospel of Jesus Christ with others is the ministry of every follower of Christ. Every believer in the church, pastors, music leaders, ushers, Bible teachers, nursery workers, Sunday morning worshipers, has the ministry of reconciliation and needs to find an expression of this responsibility through his/her local church. True followers of Christ will be compelled by the Holy Spirit to find meaningful and practical expressions for the hope that is within them (1 Peter 3:15).

PLACE
I am a member of the Body of Christ

> 1 Corinthians 12:12-14
> For as the body is one and has many members, but all the members of that one body, being many, are one body, so also is Christ. For by one Spirit we were all baptized into one body — whether Jews or Greeks, whether slaves or free — and have all been made to drink into one Spirit. For in fact the body is not one member but many.

As a believer in Christ, the Lord Jesus places me in His Body, His Church, and cherishes me as His special possession. I cannot be lost for He is in me and I am in Him (John 14:20). Jesus is my hope and my salvation. Within the church universal and local, my place is to follow Christ. When a child becomes unruly and out of line you may hear a parent say, "Child, you better find your place." Such words are a not so veiled threat for the child to change his behavior and find himself in submission to his parents or suffer the consequences. In the church, when we know our place, we no longer have to jockey for positions of power and prestige. When we know our place, conflicts and contentions subside. Unity within the Body becomes evident as each individual in the Body of Christ knows his/her place with the singular purpose of gaining and maintaining the mind of Christ (Philippians 2:1-7).

ROLE
I have a role and responsibility in the body of Christ.

My role for being on the planet is to know God and Jesus Christ (John 17:3). I come to know God and Jesus as I obey His commandments (John 14:21). This is my responsibility. Often the key to learning obedience is to practice submission. We all have to learn obedience because obedience is not natural. By submitting to the will of the Father, I evidence the same mind as Christ Who humbled Himself by becoming obedient unto death, even death on the cross (Philippians 2). The writer of Hebrews extends this idea even further when he wrote: "Though He was a Son, yet He learned obedience by the things which He suffered. And having been perfected, He became the author of eternal salvation to all who obey Him" (Hebrews 5:8-10).

Whatever position I may have (leader/follower), I must always seek to practice submission. I personally don't have a problem learning submission from God. What I really have a problem with is when God teaches me submission through someone else. It is when I am responsible to obey the command of God by being submissive to another human being that I usually find I am trying to rationalize my way out of being a follower so that I can make up my own mind about a matter. However, the way for me to fulfill my role and responsibility is through submission, and it is through submission that I, as a follower, exercise tremendous influence.

INFLUENCE
I influence others.

A surprising component of followers is the breadth of their influence. Although much of the leadership literature addresses the influence of leaders upon followers, the truth is that leaders and followers influence each other. We all influence each other. We cannot be alive on the planet and not influence each other. I address the influence of followers in the next chapter. However, never presume that followers are powerless to impact lives.

1 Thessalonians 1:6-10
And you became followers of us and of the Lord, having received the word in much affliction, with joy of the Holy Spirit, so that you became examples to all in Macedonia and Achaia who believe. For from you the word of the Lord has sounded forth, not only in Macedonia and Achaia, but also in every place. Your faith toward God has gone out, so that we do not need to say anything. For they themselves declare concerning us what manner of entry we had to you, and how you turned to God from idols to serve the living and true God, and to wait for His Son from heaven, whom He raised from the dead, *even* Jesus who delivers us from the wrath to come.

The above Scripture tells the story of how the gospel was spread throughout the region by the believers of Thessalonica becoming "followers of us and of the Lord." Turning from idols to serve (follow) the living and true God, these people probably had no idea that their simple act of following the Lord Jesus would have such a world-wide impact. Consider how many millions have read of their following over the course of 2,000 years. How many lives have been changed as a result of their response? It is a question we need to constantly ask ourselves, "How am I influencing others toward Jesus?" If I do not assume the responsibility to follow Jesus everyday in everyway, then it is likely that my life is influencing others not to follow Christ. There is no neutral ground. As I follow, I influence those around me. I desire to influence others in such as way as they might become followers of Christ.

Following Jesus' Path

Just how does one follow Christ today? An exegetical study of Luke 9:23 outlines a path all followers of Christ take as they enjoy the benefits of following Christ. After hearing Peter's answer that Jesus was "the Christ of God" (Luke 9:20), Jesus begins to explain that He must go to Jerusalem and suffer and die. Matthew records that Peter took Jesus

91

aside and rebuked Him for saying such things. In response to Peter's words, Jesus rebuked Peter saying the famous line, "Get behind Me, Satan." It is after this strong rebuke that Jesus turned to His disciples and said:

> If anyone desires to come after Me, let him deny himself, and take up his cross daily, and follow Me.

This verse of Scripture contains five important concepts that are essential in understanding how we are to follow Christ.

1. If anyone desires

The beginning point for every decision is the follower's will. When we follow Christ, we act according to our will. This requires our will to be consumed with the desires of Christ and not our own personal desires. The Holy Spirit enables the believer to will to follow, and God is glorified by the willing response of His new creation.

2. To come after Me

In the above verse, one might think the terms "come after" and "follow" are the same terms with the same meaning. However, in this verse they are distinct. The use of the word "come after" can be translated *to line up after*. When I was a child, we used to play a game called follow the leader. The point of the game is to do everything the leader does. If the leader jumps on one foot you would have to jump on one foot. If the leader jumps over a rock you would have to jump over the rock or be out of the game. Each person lines up after the leader and does exactly as the leader. I believe this is the essence of what Jesus means when he uses the term "come after." His disciples would literally follow Him, listening to every word and observing every act. Even though today it is impossible for believers to physically line up behind Christ, it is possible for followers of Christ to listen to every word and observe every act recorded in Scripture. In this way we can *line up* behind Jesus and apply the words and ways of the Lord Jesus to our lives.

One further insight to the game Follow the Leader is that when we played the game as children, we would always have to determine who would be the first leader. The choice was actually very easy. The leader would be the person in whose backyard we were playing the game. If we went to Chris' house, Chris would be the leader, same for Hank, Greg, or me. You always followed the lead of the person in whose backyard you played the game. The same is true with regard to following Christ. Every person on the planet plays in God's backyard. This is His earth, and we have no right to claim independence in what we will or will not do. We all play the game according to His rules. He is the Leader. We follow Him and no other. If we refuse to follow Him we lose.

3. Let him deny himself

An important aspect of the above phrase is to realize what Jesus did not say. Jesus did not say to deny ourselves things. He invites us to deny self. Jesus makes it clear that the heart of the person (self) is His primary concern (Matthew 23:27). If we follow Christ we must deny self. Our purpose for being on the planet is to be consumed with honoring Him from the heart. Quite simply put, if we follow Christ, we can never put our needs, our desires, and our goals and dreams in the primary position. Christ must be preeminent in all things (Colossians 1:18).

4. And take up his cross daily

Without question, the cross was the cruelest and most humiliating form of execution the Romans could think of for the day. It was the electric chair, the gas chamber, and lethal injection all wrapped up into one excruciatingly painful way to die. This is the cross. It is a place to die. And it is here that we learn to die to self. Our Leader set the example and followed the will of the Father to His cross. We must take up our cross daily and follow Him. The cross is not a one time opportunity. For followers of Christ, the cross is a daily experience of death to self and reliance upon Christ for our every need.

Think of the multitude of opportunities we have to take up our cross. The workplace is a wonderful place to die to self. How many times are we met with people who want to take advantage of us, treat us poorly, or perhaps advance over us at our expense? It is our responses to these opportunities that reveal whether or not we are dead to self and alive to Christ. The home is another place of opportunity to take up the cross. Any time you have two people in close proximity for extended periods of time you run the risk of conflict. As much as we may not like it, men and women are human and sometimes we act as fallen humanity instead of followers of Christ. On these occasions, it is our response of forgiveness and compassion that allows us to humble ourselves before our spouse and submit ourselves to each other. Finally, the church is a good place to die. There are many hurting people in the church. We sometimes cover up our hurt with a plastic smile and a phony, "I'm blessed," but underneath the façade is a heart that has been broken and emotions that have been wounded. It does not take much to have certain people in the church respond in ways that do not honor Christ. Still, it is the follower's opportunity to die to self in these instances and respond in ways that only the Holy Spirit can empower. The one who dies first is the leader.

5. And follow Me.

Jesus concludes His sentence with the words, "Follow Me." As mentioned before, this is a different Greek word than the word for "come after." This word can be translated "come alongside." Putting the different pieces of the verse together, the picture I have in my mind is a progression of personal intimacy with the Savior. Willing followers line up their lives with the Savior as the Bible reveals His words and actions beginning a journey of walking in the same path with Jesus, following His lead in every endeavor. In the process, the providence of the Lord provides ample opportunity for the follower to experience joys and blessings, as well as endure hardships and disappointments. Each day the follower is given opportunities to die to self and glorify the Lord through every event. It is in this process that the followers one day realize their walk with Jesus is not one of lock-step obedience to His commands but rather a relationship of willing love and abandonment to Him. It is as if the followers are walking alongside the Lord Jesus with His arms around their shoulders, whispering to them intimate details of Himself and His love which compels these followers to love and obey Him even more.

Such is the progression of followers. They take on the persona of the One whom they follow. They are bold, yet humble; strong, yet weak; assertive, yet submissive. In all things they hold their purpose as a treasure, to honor the One whom they love more than life itself, their leader, the Lord Jesus Christ.

Conclusion

As you think about your own journey of following the Savior and developing a biblical follower identity, I share with you the words of G. D. Watson (1845-1924).[2] I first read them as a young seminary student and today these words still challenge me to be the follower of Christ I know I should be. Through the power of God's Spirit and His process of sanctification, let us pray and act in such a way that God will be glorified through our lives.

Others May... You Cannot

If God has called you to be really like Jesus he will draw you into a life of crucifixion and humility, and put upon you such demands of obedience, that you will not be able to follow other people, or measure yourself by other Christians, and in many ways he will seem to let other people do things which he will not let you do.

Other Christians and ministers who seem very religious and useful, may push themselves, pull wires, and work schemes to carry out their plans, but you cannot do it, and if you attempt it, you will meet with such failure and rebuke from the Lord as to make you sorely penitent.

Others may boast of themselves, of their work, of their success, of their writings, but the Holy Spirit will not allow you to do any such thing, and if you begin it, he will lead you into some deep mortification that will make you despise yourself and all your good works.

Other may be allowed to succeed in making money, or may have a legacy left to them, but it is likely God will keep you poor, because he wants you to have something far better than gold, namely, a helpless dependence upon him, that he may have the privilege of supplying your needs day by day out of an unseen treasury.

The Lord may let others be honored and put forward, and keep you hidden in obscurity, because he wants to produce some choice fragrant fruit for his coming glory, which can only be produced in the shade. He may let others be great, but keep you small. He may let others do a work for him and get the credit for it, but he will make you work and toil on without knowing how much you are doing, and then to make your work still more precious he may let others get credit for the work which you have done, and thus make your reward ten times greater when Jesus comes.

The Holy Spirit will put a strict watch over you, with a jealous love, and will rebuke you for little words and feelings or for wasting your time, which other Christians never feel distressed over. So make up your mind that God is an infinite Sovereign, and has a right to do as he pleases with his own. He may not explain to you a thousand things which puzzle your reason in his dealings with you, but if you absolutely sell yourself to be his love slave, he will wrap you up in a jealous love, and bestow upon you many blessing which come only to those who are in the inner circle.

Settle it forever, then, that you are to deal directly with the Holy Sprit and that He is to have the privilege of tying your tongue, or chaining your hand, or closing you eyes, in ways that he does not seem to use with others. Now, when you are so possessed with the living God that you are, in your secret heart, pleased and delighted over this peculiar, personal, private, jealous guardianship and management of the Holy Spirit over your life, you will have found the vestibule of Heaven.

Follower Identity: The Freedom to Be

The Follower Paradox
- Find Life by Losing It
- Be Strong by Becoming Weak
- Receive by Giving
- Impact the World by Following

Personalize
- Identity
- Title
- Ministry
- Place
- Role
- Influence

Following Jesus' Path
- If anyone desires
- To come after Me
- Let him deny himself
- And take up his cross
- And follow Me

Others May… You Cannot

Chapter 5

The Follower's Influence

One of the most surprising aspects of Follower First thinking is the amount of influence followers have within organizations. For the past 30 years we have been teaching leaders that "everything rises and falls on leadership," and such statements have gone largely unchallenged. The reason for such uncritical thinking may be that in our western culture we are programmed to believe leaders are better and have the power. This assessment is reinforced through the media, personal experience, as well as much of the literature we read.

In this chapter, I challenge the prevailing thinking regarding leaders being the *sine qua non* of the organization. Joseph Rost and others (Chapter 3) have challenged the linear aspect of the leader-follower relationship by focusing on the process of leadership and the interdependence of each responsible party in the organization. Highlighting the influence that followers have within an organization can be illustrated by the following two diagrams.

Figure 4 illustrates the normal organizational chart for a simple hierarchical organization. The leader is at the top and everyone else is considered a follower. It is assumed that the leader at the top holds influence over all others in the chart. What the leader does impacts everyone within the alignment. Thus, if everything rises and falls on the leader, as is often preached, then an assumption is being made that the followers are merely responders to the leader and have no initiative of their own. However, what if the follower with the X drawn through the box decides that he or she does not want to play that game anymore? To debunk the "everything rises and falls on leadership" myth, let us turn our attention to Figure 5.

As you can see, the result of the follower's actions turns the entire organization upside down. Unfortunately, churches experience this type of upheaval regularly. The leader may have been a good leader. The leader may have performed his duties in textbook fashion, yet the results are not exponential growth but chaos and confusion. Such a scenario prompts pastors and church leaders to leave the ministry everyday thinking they are failures when they may have been leading exactly as they should have been as faithful followers of the Lord Jesus Christ. The reason for the failure may not have been a crisis of leading but, as in this case, a crisis of following. Everything does NOT rise and fall on leadership.

As a young pastor, I had the privilege of hearing Dr. Charles Stanley of the First Baptist Church in Atlanta give some sage advice that I did not embrace until the latter part of my pastoral ministry. I can't remember the exact quote, but the substance of his remarks was that, it doesn't matter how good a pastor you are or how good a preacher you are, if the church does not want to grow, it will not grow. This simple fact is the 800 pound gorilla in leadership teaching that few are willing to recognize.

Without question leaders influence those around them. They have the position and usually the organizational authority to direct the organization. However, these two illustrations graphically illustrate how refusing to recognize the influence of followers can lead to total disarray and confusion.

Figure 4: Normal Organizational Structure

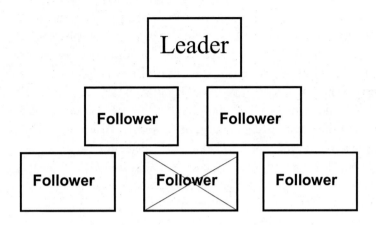

Figure 5: Result of Follower Resistance

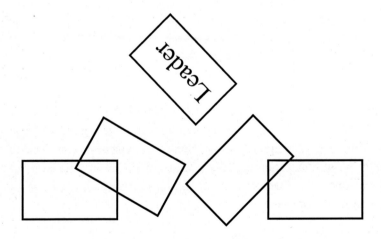

Someone may suggest that if the leader in these figures had been a better leader with better skills the dissenting follower would not have pulled out. Such a contention can not be proven because leading and following are not the linear cause and effect scientific process that much leadership literature presupposes. Leadership, to reiterate Joseph Rost, is an interdependent relationship between a leader and a follower in which there must be cooperation or leadership does not exist.

There is no guarantee that good leading will result in good following. It may increase the odds, but followers always have the choice of whether or not they will follow the lead of the leader. A follower has a will that is free to act on its own. Guided by a biblical ethic, followers of Christ can decide whether of not the leader is acting in a God-honoring manner and choose to respond accordingly. By using a leader style that respects the role of the follower, and/or by embracing the Following-Leader style (Chapter 6), leaders can influence followers to participate in the life of the church and become an integral part of the church's mission. The choice, however, remains with the follower.

Leaders and followers need to realize the power and influence followers have within the organization. Followers within any organization and especially the church have tremendous responsibilities to act in ways that preserve the unity of the Spirit in the bond of peace (Ephesians 4:3). Followers need to be taught that the casual word, the off comment to another, the occasional speculation about the integrity of the leader, can be fatal to the overall mission of the church. Consider Paul's teaching to the church when he instructs the church to "quit devouring one another" (Galatians 5:15). From the context it is evident Paul is talking to the followers of Christ whether they are leaders or followers. By finding common ground as fellow followers with different responsibilities, the participants in the church organization can seek to overcome the common principles of leading through authority and power and instead find the freedom to act according to the teaching of responsibility and submission.

Authority and Power

The concept of authority is often misused and misunderstood in the church. This confusion results from misunderstanding the biblical teaching regarding authority, who has it, how it is distributed through the church, and the limits of authority within the church organization. An in-depth study of the concept is outside the purview of this book. However, I encourage you to study it further.[1]

From an organizational perspective, authority is a person's legitimate power "to influence others because of the position within the organization that person holds."[2] Persons within the organization agree to recognize that the person occupying a particular position within the organization has the right to influence others solely because of the position held. Organizational authority has the following characteristics:

1. *It is vested in a person's position.* An individual has authority because of the position he/she holds, not because of any specific personal characteristics.
2. *It is accepted by subordinates.* The individual... can gain compliance because he or she has a legitimate right.
3. *Authority is used vertically.* Authority flows from the top down in the hierarchy of an organization.[3]

A biblical perspective understands that all authority is vested in God. His authority is intrinsic, unconditional, and absolute (Psalms 29:10; Isaiah 40:1).[4] As God in the flesh, Jesus introduces the Great Commission with the words, "All authority has been given to Me in heaven and on earth" (Matthew 28:18). In the text the word authority translates the Greek word *exousia* which in other texts is translated power.[5] This authority is emphasized by the Apostle Paul when He wrote in Colossians 2:8-10:

> Beware lest anyone cheat you through philosophy and empty deceit, according to the tradition of men, according to the basic principles of the world, and not according to Christ. For in Him

dwells all the fullness of the Godhead bodily; and you are complete in Him, who is the head of all principality and power.

All human or organizational authority is derived from God and historically recognized through certain societal constructs:

Governments

Romans 13:1-7
Let every soul be subject to the governing authorities. For there is no authority except from God, and the authorities that exist are appointed by God. Therefore whoever resists the authority resists the ordinance of God, and those who resist will bring judgment on themselves. For rulers are not a terror to good works, but to evil. Do you want to be unafraid of the authority? Do what is good, and you will have praise from the same. For he is God's minister to you for good. But if you do evil, be afraid; for he does not bear the sword in vain; for he is God's minister, an avenger to execute wrath on him who practices evil. Therefore you must be subject, not only because of wrath but also for conscience' sake. For because of this you also pay taxes, for they are God's ministers attending continually to this very thing. Render therefore to all their due: taxes to whom taxes are due, customs to whom customs, fear to whom fear, honor to whom honor.

Bondservants and Masters

Ephesians 6:5-9
Bondservants, be obedient to those who are your masters according to the flesh, with fear and trembling, in sincerity of heart, as to Christ; not with eyeservice, as men-pleasers, but as bondservants of Christ, doing the will of God from the heart, with goodwill doing service, as to the Lord, and not to men, knowing that whatever good anyone does, he will receive the same from the Lord, whether he is a slave or free. And you, masters, do the same things to them, giving up threatening,

knowing that your own Master also is in heaven, and there is no partiality with Him.

Parents

Ephesians 6:1-4
Children, obey your parents in the Lord, for this is right. "Honor your father and mother," which is the first commandment with promise: "that it may be well with you and you may live long on the earth." And you, fathers, do not provoke your children to wrath, but bring them up in the training and admonition of the Lord.

Elders

Hebrews 13:7 & 17
Remember those who rule over you, who have spoken the word of God to you, whose faith follow, considering the outcome of their conduct. 17 Obey those who rule over you, and be submissive, for they watch out for your souls, as those who must give account. Let them do so with joy and not with grief, for that would be unprofitable for you.

It is important to realize that a person's position of authority does not necessarily mean that the person has power to influence others. This reality stems from the fact that,

Power is not an attribute of a particular person. Rather, it is an aspect of the relationship that exists between two (or more) people. No individual or group can have power in isolation; power must exist in relation to some other person or group. If A has power over B, it is, in part, because B is willing for that to be an aspect of the relationship between them. If and when B no longer desires that to be part of the relationship with A, A will no longer have power over B and no longer be able to influence B's behavior. Thus obtaining, maintaining, and using power are all essential to influencing the behavior of people in organizational settings.[6]

One key point from the above quote is that power is not granted because of position. Power is **obtained** through a relationship between the leader and the follower. Although a person's power may be legitimized because of their position of authority, that person's authority to tell another person to perform a task does not guarantee they have the power to make the person perform the task. This is one point that needs to be clarified in the church, especially as it relates to the concept of pastoral authority.

Pastoral Authority

Pastoral authority is a concept that derives its merit from the biblical injunction for the members of the church to be submissive to those who have oversight of the church (Hebrews 13:17). The construct gives biblical authority to a pastor of a local church to equip the saints so that the members of that church follow his lead with regard to how the church should function and operate in fulfilling God's purpose according to the Scripture. This concept is more common in churches with congregational polity as opposed to those with elders. There is some debate regarding the operation of such authority within the church. However, I mention it here as a means to show how a Follower First philosophy enhances the position of the lead pastor of a church without the pastor having to rely upon this authority construct. In my experience, those pastors who focus on their pastoral authority often extend the scope of such authority beyond what Scripture allows. Such an expansion usually results in: (a) the congregation assenting to the desires of the pastor, (b) the congregation rebelling against the desires of the pastor, (c) the congregation half-heartedly complying with the desires while a growing dislike of the pastor simmers within the body making the life of the pastor and his family extremely difficult, or (d) the extra burden of assuming responsibilities not outlined in the Scriptures become unbearable and the pastor leaves the ministry.

Most members of a church would not debate the clear teaching that Jesus is the head of the church (Colossians 2:10). Where the difficulty is sometimes evidenced is when the pastor, ruling elders, or similar individuals within the church, claim authority that has not been scripturally given to them.

What then does the Bible teach with regard to a pastor's authority? Alex Montoya presents the following summation:

> The pastor, then, is by his calling a spiritual leader. His calling comes from God. His allotment is the spiritual oversight of a Sprit-led body of believers (1 Peter 5:3; cf. 2:5-10). His qualifications for holding office are spiritual (1 Timothy 3:1-8). His methods for ministering are spiritual (Acts 6:4; 2 Corinthians 10:4; 2 Timothy 4:1-4). His accountability (Hebrews 13:17) and rewards are spiritual (2 Timothy 4:8; 1 Peter 5:4).[7]

The Bible makes it clear that the primary concern for leaders in the church is that the leader be a spiritual leader with godly character. Pastors/elders are never to "lord" (Matthew 20:25) their position over the members of the congregation. This is made clear by James Means when he wrote,

> Never are church leaders to think of their status as lordship, but as servanthood. Leaders are not selected so that they might have dominion over the body of believers, but that there might be guidance in spiritual matters by qualified, godly individuals under the lordship of Christ. Therefore, however we interpret the words rule, direct, obey and submit, they cannot be interpreted in a way that gives leaders the kind of authority that the rulers of the Gentiles had, or that officials exercise in the secular world.[8]

Aubrey Malphurs suggests it is the ability of the pastor to follow that gives the pastor insight into how authority is exercised within the church. Malphurs stated,

> A primary requirement for a leader in the church is the ability to follow; that is, following Christ by following other God-given authorities…As the church develops leaders, it must observe how emerging leaders respond to authority. The ability to be under authority should drive who emerges as leaders and when

they emerge…The assessment of this quality is important for leaders at every level….[9]

Malphurs supports the Follower First philosophy by reminding leaders it is who they follow and how they follow that determines the influence one has, especially within the church. Pastors must understand they are under the authority of the Lord Jesus Christ and the Scriptures and regularly communicate this understanding to the members of the church. The pastor's humility and submission to Christ will communicate a Follower First philosophy that will act as a catalyst to the church body, resulting in a corporate submission to Christ.

Even though the pastor operates within the church in a position of organizational authority, he cannot hope to lead (influence) others solely from this position. Pastoral authority can not simply be a function of a position in the church. The pastor's sense of authority must be geared toward the spiritual aspects of intimacy with Jesus. Robert Clinton addressed this authority when he wrote,

> Spiritual authority is not a goal but rather a byproduct. It is a delegated authority that comes from God. It is the major power base of a leader who has learned God's lessons during maturity processing. Leaders have various power bases that give credence to their ability. Spiritual authority comes out of experience with God. A leader does not seek spiritual authority; a leader seeks to know God. Maturity processing enhances this desire to know God. Spiritual authority results from a leader's experience with God.[10]

Although the pastor is responsible before God as one who will give an account for those under his charge, the pastor will only give an account of his personal faithfulness in carrying out the **biblical** duties and responsibilities of the pastor, namely to teach/preach the Word of God (2 Timothy 4:2), do the work of an evangelist (2 Timothy 4:5), and equip the saints for the work of the ministry (Ephesians 4:12). Pastoral authority does not extend to an expectation that the people in the church are required to follow the pastor in any and every project or ministry that he may present. It may be controversial to say, but followers are not required by God to obey pastors as they lead in building programs, or paying off debt, or any number of good and worthwhile projects and plans. Such actions are ancillary to the primary role of the pastor and do not carry biblical authority.

When I am teaching this section, I will ask the class to imagine I am their pastor. I then hold my Bible over my head as a symbolic representation of my submission to the authority of Christ and the Word of God. While holding my Bible over my head, I will then inform them that their duty as followers is to listen and heed the authority of what I say as pastor, as long as I am speaking the "thus says the Lord" of the Word of God. I will then move the Bible from over my head and hold it out to the side. At this point I tell the class that from this position I no longer hold biblical authority but, taking my place as a fellow member of the church, serve as a consultant to the Body of Christ. My training, expertise, and experiences may help the church fulfill her purpose, but at this point I do not speak "thus says the Lord," and the church is not required to listen or heed what I say. I might also add that, as the pastor of the church, God does not hold me responsible for the obedience or disobedience of the individual members of the church or the corporate actions of the church regarding these programs or plans. As a pastor, God will hold me responsible for how I equipped the saints to do the work of the ministry. Each follower of Christ is responsible before God for the responsibilities God has assigned to him or her in the Word. It may not be good English, but it makes sense: *I am only responsible for what I'm responsible for.*

This understanding serves to free the pastor from self-imposed pressures brought about by some leadership teachings that imply the pastor is solely responsible for the growth of the church. Paul's admonition to Timothy was, "Preach the Word..." (2 Timothy 4:2) and "[equip] the saints" (Ephesians 4:12). As we have studied, faithfully preaching the Bible and equipping people for works of service in the church do not always result in church growth. In fact, if the follower capacity of the members of the church is low, faithfully preaching and teaching the Bible results in anger, disunity, and stagnation. The world may view such a church as having poor leadership. However, in the eyes of the Lord, such a pastor has remained faithful in fulfilling his biblical responsibilities. Whatever our place of responsibility within the church, let us always remember Paul's words in 1 Corinthians 3:5-9:

> What, after all, is Apollos? And what is Paul? Only servants, through whom you came to believe-as the Lord has assigned to each his task. I planted the seed, Apollos watered it, but God made it grow. So neither he who plants nor he who waters is anything, but only God, who makes things grow. The man who plants and the man who waters have one purpose, and each will be rewarded according to his own labor. For we are God's fellow workers; you are God's field, God's building.

Let me at this point direct an important caveat to those with leader responsibilities in the church who are not fulltime ministerial staff. Although the pastor/elders operate as consultants to the church when planning events, outreaches, buildings, etc., it is important for the members of the church to realize that these pastors and staff members eat, drink, sleep, and die a thousand deaths trying to figure out ways for the church to fulfill her mission. I think I can speak for many pastors when I say that it is extremely disheartening, after having planned and prepared for months to present a plan to the church leaders only to have it rejected out of hand by a group that is not at the church everyday of the week, are not constantly pressed by the needs of the ministry, and often do not have a big picture of the need for certain actions.

As I have stated previously, there is no biblical mandate stating that church members are required to agree with every plan the pastor or leader team presents. However, I would urge every member to realize that cavalier attitudes or power plays to show the pastor who is in charge and other worldly expressions of power and control are extremely dangerous to those who might play these political games within the church.

As followers realize their power to act or not act, it is wise to listen carefully to those who are your spiritual leaders even when they are speaking outside the realm of their biblical authority. Many pastors have read, studied, and prepared themselves to act in the best interest of the longevity and viability of the church. What they present may be new to you, but I can almost guarantee that the plans and ideas are not new to them. They have been prayed over, cried over, sweated over, and in come cases even bled over all for the sake of seeking to know the will of God in the matter. A spirit of mutual respect is highly recommended. Be certain that if you have reservations regarding following your pastors, that your reservations are presented with the same prayed over, cried over, bled over desire to know the will of God. With a mutual desire to follow the will of God, and rejecting political infighting and power plays, much can be accomplished through the follower-leader relationship.

God holds the pastor/elder responsible for the accurate teaching, shepherding, and equipping of the saints in the Word of God. Followers are responsible to obey and respect those who hold positions of biblical authority within the church as these people carry out their God-given responsibilities. Followers are responsible to have teachable hearts for the Word of God. Followers are to join with the pastor/elder in making disciples of all nations. Followers are to make themselves available to be equipped for the work of service, and they can do this work as unto the Lord and not as unto men. It is here that followers can let the leaders lead with joy because the end result will be a benefit for all.

Sad but true, many a young or uninformed pastor has made his life and those around him miserable thinking that his pastoral authority is what is going to influence others. Such ideas are tolerated only for a short period of time before the congregation begins to resist. Pastors/elders need to understand that influence is the result of relationships. It is through these relationships that certain types of power can be exercised that influence others.[11]

Types of Power

Reward Power

Reward power is usually addressed from the perspective that the leader has an ability to reward the compliance of followers. I would quickly add that followers also have reward power in rewarding leaders with their following. Reward power establishes a type of exchange relationship or a transaction whereby the leader agrees to offer a certain reward in exchange for the compliance of the follower. As in all sources of power, the follower may agree with this reward or may choose not to comply.

In the church, reward power may be positively manifested through the leaders acknowledging individuals for jobs well done or showing appreciation for service within the church. It has been my observation that consistently showing gratitude to those who work within the church both at a paid and especially at a volunteer level is gravely lacking. Additionally, I have seen churches in which followers rarely if ever show any appreciation for their leaders except once a year when the newly established pastor appreciation month roles around. Followers would do well to embrace Paul's admonition in 1 Timothy 5:17-19, "Let the elders who rule well be counted worthy of double honor, especially those who labor in the word and doctrine. For the Scripture says, 'You shall not muzzle an ox while it treads out the grain,' and, 'The laborer is worthy of his wages'." Showing appreciation to pastors and other leaders who consistently serve the Lord by ministering and serving the Body of Christ never dishonors God.

Senior pastors can follow these same guidelines. First, senior pastors and every staff member need to remember to appreciate their spouse. There is no more important person than your spouse. Guard this relationship and constantly show your spouse your appreciation for all they do to support you. Additionally, except for their spouse, there are no more important people to a senior pastor than those who work in fulltime ministry positions alongside him and those who serve in administrative areas of service. Take the time to appreciate your staff. Go to meals together. Find the time to recreate together. Support them and serve them. Reward their loyalty to you by being loyal. Keep confidences. Be a friend. These followers who follow Christ and you don't require much except your love. Give it to them.

For all the positives rewarding people may have, there are negatives. These occur when the leader chooses to withhold rewards or extend rewards for the purpose of manipulating people to comply with requests. This type of exchange system establishes an implied contract in which the leader only rewards behaviors that comply with the leader's stated desires. Such theories of leadership are firmly rooted in business organizations in which paychecks are used as rewards for services rendered. Such actions may not be as overt in the church, but contingencies can be established between leaders and followers, especially as it regards funding special projects within the church. For example, if a member decides to help the pastor with a project with a large some of money, there may be an implied expectation that in the future that member would be rewarded with some special favor. On these occasions, gifts ostensibly given to the Lord through the church actually become bribes for future favors. As followers of Christ, we must seek to alleviate doing business in this way. We will address this *quid pro quo* relationship later.

One important aspect for followers and leaders to remember is all such rewards are but temporal expressions. The spiritual reality is that the greatest and most precious reward a leader or follower can give to another is faithful service to the Lord Jesus. As pastors accurately teach and preach the Word of God, as elders oversee matters of the church humbly and with servant hearts, as followers willingly follow, trusting the leading of the Lord through their leaders, the Body is blessed, healthy, and able to fulfill its mission and vision of making disciples of all nations.

Coercive Power

Coercive power is based upon the leader's ability to punish followers for non-compliance with requests. This may be the type of power the Lord Jesus spoke of when He said in Matthew 20:25-28,

> You know that the rulers of the Gentiles lord it over them, and their great men exercise authority over them. It is not so among you, but whoever wishes to become great among you shall be your servant, and whoever wishes to be first among you shall be your slave; just as the Son of Man did not come to be served, but to serve, and to give His life a ransom for many.

In this text the phrase "lord it over" has the idea of control or subjugation.[12] It is clear that Jesus does not want His followers assuming they can coerce people into obedience.

Many times within the church, coercive power is implemented in order to cajole people into certain behaviors. Leaders may sometimes use guilt manipulation in sermons to try and emotionally move the people to comply with what the Bible commands or, even more egregious, to get the church to agree with their particular plan for the church. It is sometimes too easy for leaders to succumb to using language that implies, "If you don't stand with this plan, you will be standing against the will of God." Even more destructive is for the leader to begin thinking that those who disagree with his plan must be of the devil. Such thoughts and actions are not those of a leader, but a manipulator, and an authoritarian. Characteristically, in Ephesians 6:5-9, Paul identifies a coercive leader-follower relationship as that between a slave owner and a bond slave and instructs both to cease from such destructive behaviors:

> Bondservants, be obedient to those who are your masters according to the flesh, with fear and trembling, in sincerity of heart, as to Christ; not with eye-service, as men-pleasers, but as bondservants of Christ, doing the will of God from the heart, with goodwill doing service, as to the Lord, and not to men, knowing that whatever good anyone does, he will receive the same from the Lord, whether he is a slave or free. And you, masters, do the same things to them, giving up threatening, knowing that your own Master also is in heaven, and there is no partiality with Him.

Astute followers have the capacity to perceive coercive behaviors and to choose not to comply. Taking up the courageous follower mantle, followers need to address coercive behaviors with the leader, individually, privately, and gently. It may be that the leader is unaware of his/her manipulative tendencies. However, in the case of the leader who intentionally uses coercive power, followers can put him/her on notice that they are aware of what he/she is doing and will not respond positively to continuous coercive techniques.

Although coercive power usually resides in the person who holds the position of leader, followers also have a degree of what I call passive coercive power by choosing to respond or not to respond. As we have already shown, follower response can either make the leader or break the leader. If followers use their responses as manipulative weapons to try and direct the actions of the leader, they are using a form of passive coercive power to move the leader in a desired direction. Such actions produce nothing but conflict. Personal relationships in the church usually suffer while productive ministry ceases. Open communication between leader and follower without speculation or assumption on either party's part is necessary for the church to remain healthy and vibrant.

Expert Power

Expert power rests with those who may have a particular expertise. Some pastors have a gift of preaching. Others may have a gift of administration. It is through these gifts, and others, that the pastor can influence those around him. Followers as well have a form of expert power. As I have observed decision making in the church, coming to a decision is vested with a small group of individuals to the exclusion of the larger church body. Although I recognize the functional benefits of such a decision making system, at the initial stages of the decision making process, the Follower First philosophy encourages leaders to include as many minds as possible. By seeking the genius of the whole, the expertise of one who could really make a difference may be added to the decision making process. Whether leader or follower, expert power needs to be held with an attitude of humility if it is to be honoring to God. The expertise must be understood as a stewardship from God for His glory and the benefit of the Body of Christ. Such expertise should be used to influence others toward greater obedience to God and not used to aggrandize self or for personal advantage.

Referent Power

This type of power rests with the charisma of the individual leader or follower and is based on the person's character and integrity. Trust is built between the leader and the follower as each exercises integrity and competence over time. The trust formed through this mutually interdependent relationship creates a powerful dynamic that allows both leader and follower to operate at high levels of performance and productivity. Both follower and leader are to be persons of the highest character and integrity. In other words, as a Follower First, both leader and follower are to manifest the character and integrity of Christ basing all decisions on the core values found in the Scriptures.

Structural Power

Structural power "results from the nature of the organizational social system rather than from attributes of an individual."[13] That is, the structure of the organization determines who has the authority to make the decision. It is the structure that determines a person's specific tasks and responsibilities and thus, lends the commensurate power and authority for carrying out those prescribed tasks.

Within the church there is specific structure with regard to bishops, pastors, elders, and deacons. Leaders who hold these offices within the church are bound by Scripture to fulfill the responsibilities given to them by the Lord, who is the Head of the church. As previously stated, officers of the church need to perceive that they are followers of Christ and obedient to His prescribed duties and responsibilities. The officers need to be aware of over-stepping their place within the church structure so as not to assume power and authority not specifically given by the Scripture.

Although rarely recognized, persons who hold the position of follower within an organization have a type of structural power. The hierarchical structure of most organizations is built upon a foundation of followers. Any engineer knows that a structure is only as stable as its foundation. In the church, the Lord Jesus Christ serves as the "chief cornerstone" upon which the entire body rests (Acts 4:11). As the perfect follower, Jesus establishes His church upon the expectation that those who believe in Him will follow His Word and obey His commands. To have hierarchical positions within the church organization and have people in those positions who do not follow Christ is to sabotage the very purpose for the existence of the church. The church was established to follow Christ. Structural power without following Christ becomes an exercise of human aggrandizement that scandalizes the name and character of Christ before the world.

Resource Power

Resource power resides with the person who has access to resources (money, relationships, technology, etc.) needed by the ministry in order to fulfill its mission. It is likely that a new pastor entering a congregation will have some resource power. However, it is more likely that members of the congregation or longer term staff members will have more of this type of power.

The ministry is filled with horror stories of the abuse of this type of power. There may be a wealthy person within the church who uses his resources to influence decisions within the church either through giving gifts or withholding them. Other persons may have access to individuals whom they believe can help the church with its mission, but such help is only forthcoming with conditions of advancement or recognition. Such abuses of this type of power are expressly prohibited within the church as written in James 2:2-9:

> Suppose a man comes into your meeting wearing a gold ring and fine clothes, and a poor man in shabby clothes also comes in. If you show special attention to the man wearing fine clothes and say, "Here's a good seat for you," but say to the poor man, "You stand there" or "Sit on the floor by my feet," have you not discriminated among yourselves and become judges with evil thoughts? Listen, my dear brothers: Has not God chosen those who are poor in the eyes of the world to be rich in faith and to

inherit the kingdom he promised those who love him? But you have insulted the poor. Is it not the rich who are exploiting you? Are they not the ones who are dragging you into court? Are they not the ones who are slandering the noble name of him to whom you belong? If you really keep the royal law found in Scripture, "Love your neighbor as yourself," you are doing right. But if you show favoritism, you sin and are convicted by the law as lawbreakers.

The correct use of resource power would be for a person to realize that he/she is a steward of all that God has given. Church leaders especially need to recognize that serving the church is a stewardship. As Paul relates in 1 Corinthians 4: 1-5:

> Let a man so consider us, as servants of Christ and stewards of the mysteries of God. Moreover it is required in stewards that one be found faithful. But with me it is a very small thing that I should be judged by you or by a human court. In fact, I do not even judge myself. For I know of nothing against myself, yet I am not justified by this; but He who judges me is the Lord. Therefore judge nothing before the time, until the Lord comes, who will both bring to light the hidden things of darkness and reveal the counsels of the hearts. Then each one's praise will come from God.

Resource power can be a tremendous blessing to the church when exercised in humility. All church ministries need resources. Those whom God has blessed with financial resources are a blessing to the church. For the person with resource power, giving becomes a way for them to honor the Lord Jesus by following Him. In this respect, all members of the church can have the joy of giving to the Lord regardless of how much or how little they give. Jesus is honored by the followers' desire to give. God is the one who sees the true gift of the heart.

Information Power

Similar to resource power, information power exists because there are those within the organization who may have knowledge about important matters that others within the organization do not. Such knowledge can, in many cases, mean the difference between success and failure. Access to this type of knowledge is crucial in decision making. Therefore, it is important to identify those who wield this power within the organization. Many times such knowledge may abide with those who have been with the organization for long periods of time. The willingness to share such information with a new leader is a tremendous asset and blessing to the leader.

Because of its similarity to resource power, those with information power must guard against being deceptive with the information they possess. The rationalization of what are termed white lies, and/or not telling all the truth about a matter are serious threats to the integrity of any organization, especially the church. The church operates on the basis of truth, both the truth of the gospel and truth speaking to one another. Paul emphasizes speaking this gospel of truth in Ephesians 4:11-16:

> It was he who gave some to be apostles, some to be prophets, some to be evangelists, and some to be pastors and teachers, to prepare God's people for works of service, so that the body of Christ may be built up until we all reach unity in the faith and in the knowledge of the Son of God and become mature, attaining to the whole measure of the fullness of Christ. Then we will no longer be infants, tossed back and forth by the waves, and blown here and there by every wind of teaching and by the cunning and craftiness of men in their deceitful scheming. Instead, speaking the truth in love, we will in all things grow up into him who is the Head, that is, Christ. From him the whole body, joined and held together by every supporting ligament, grows and builds itself up in love, as each part does its work. [14]

It is inconceivable that using information to gain an advantage over others would be acceptable in the church. This is why James said that you should "let your yes, be yes, and your no, no; so that you may not fall under judgment" (James 5:12).

Power from the Follower's Perspective

It is sometimes assumed that power is something leaders have and followers do not. Upon closer inspection we can see that followers do indeed have power within organizations and this is even more pronounced in churches. The following is a recapitulation of some of the ideas previously mentioned regarding how followers can understand their influential role within the church.

Reward Power

Each time a follower decides to do something a leader suggests, the follower is rewarding the leader with his or her own life. Followers can reward leaders with speaking the truth, sharing information, being available when needed, being responsible for activities, and most everything else you can think of that a leader would do.

Coercive Power

Coercive power is characterized by the ability to punish non-compliance. When viewed from a follower perspective, if a follower knows that a leader must have a project finished, the follower can punish the leader by not completing work, misdirecting effort, or not telling the truth. This may result in the follower being punished but the damage will have already been done. To think that followers have no coercive power is naïve.

Expert Power

Followers can be experts at anything. Unless respected and appreciated, followers may simply remain quiet about their expertise. If the follower knows that he or she will not be given credit for an idea or a solution, he or she may decide to keep the expertise to themselves. Conversely, followers who seek to follow and honor God will give their expertise to projects without thought of seeking glory for themselves.

Referent Power

The integrity and character of a follower has tremendous impact upon the leader. Leaders need those whom they can trust. By speaking the truth to the leader, the follower can become indispensible to the success and productivity of the church.

Structural Power

The essence of the church is based upon the corner stone of Jesus Christ and His following the will of the Father. Followers are the source through which every ministry of the church is accomplished.

Resource Power

Followers with resources can be a great help to the ministry. Understanding their role as a steward of that which God has given, followers can give so that others might benefit. Resources are not necessarily financial but can be a wide range of important resources to the leader and the church. By withholding resources, followers can short-circuit the efforts of any leader and may be able to do so without the leader even knowing. Positively, the follower with resource power and the right attitude to exercise it can be a great help.

Information Power

Follower lines of social interaction are vast and varied within the organization. In most situations, because of the title and position of the leader, there is little interaction with the *normal* people in the organization. Yet, it is these people who interact and cooperate with one another to make certain the organization continues to function smoothly. Followers hold vast knowledge of people within the organization. Giving and withholding information important to the leader or giving partial or errant information to the leader can do grave damage to the effectiveness of the church. With such power, it is important for followers to remember the words of Paul in Philippians 2:3-4, "Let nothing be done through selfish ambition or conceit, but in lowliness of mind let each esteem others better than himself. Let each of you look out not only for his own interests, but also for the interests of others."

Unless and until leaders understand the inherent power that followers have within the organization, they will never be able to fully utilize the vast resources, expertise, information, and personal integrity available through the followers. To put it more bluntly, if all leaders seek to do is develop people into leaders because they, the current leaders, think certain people have the qualities it takes for being a leader and leave the vast numbers of followers in the organization alone, the leaders, the churches, and other organizations will lose. If there is no change, 20% of the workers will continue to do 80% of the work because the followers, the other 80% of the people, have not been respected, equipped, and taught the responsibilities of being a follower of Christ.

Quid Pro Quo

One of the most destructive philosophies operating in the church today is the idea of the *quid pro quo*, a Latin term for "what for what" or "something for something".[15] The basis of the phrase is to give something of value for something of value. Colloquially, we might speak of, "one hand washing the other," or, "I'll scratch your back if you scratch mine." As a pastor, I was often confronted by this type of thinking when dealing with business men and women. The reason for this is that the business world operates on the idea of the exchange. The thought is, "I'll do for you and then you can do for me." As a young pastor, I was somewhat naïve about all this and found myself confronted by many who had hard feelings against me because I would not return the favor at a later time. They would remind me about votes that were taken in meetings and behind the scenes dealings on my behalf so that my agenda could be passed, and now it was my turn to do what the giver of the favor wanted me to do for them. When I refused, I was accused of not "playing the game."

Such exchanges within the church are the antithesis of the grace of God which was given to purchase and establish the church. Grace, God's *unmerited* favor, requires nothing on the part of the recipient. When God gives, He gives not as a result of our merit/works or even our future merit/works. God gives because He chooses to. It is this organizational culture of grace in which the church must operate if it is to accurately communicate the glory of God to the world. Unfortunately, and to the great peril of the church, leaders have adopted this ungodly philosophy of pay to play by which deals are struck and decisions are made. Grace is forgotten and a favor-based system of power, persuasion, and bribery takes its place. There is no longer a, "yes." There is a, "yes, if you will do this for me." The "what have you done for me lately" philosophy begins to warp the very foundation of the church and decisions are no longer based upon biblical criteria but rather a sense of entitlement and self-centeredness. Concerns for Jesus and His kingdom work are undermined for the present obtaining of temporary power and privilege. The organization devolves into a political system in which power brokers influence for their own cause, their own group, or even for their own personal benefit. We cannot allow such thinking or actions to permeate the church any longer.

What will it take to change the prevailing *quid pro quo* culture? Change will require followers of Christ willing to be misunderstood and even taken advantage of by those operating within this system. It will require followers willing to confront ungodly practices within the church and possibly be ostracized by others. It will require courageous followers with a spiritual integrity and love for Christ that cannot and will not be compromised. It will require followers of Christ who cannot be bought. A popular adage within the business world is "everyone has their price." At what price have we sold the church culture of grace for a business culture of conditions and exchanges? Those followers of Christ who wish to recover the culture of grace will surely pay a price by being misunderstood and even thought a poor leader. Are you willing?

Responses

Regardless of the power that is exerted in the follower-leader relationship, we must never forget that each person in this leadership dance has the power of his or her own decision. There are three basic responses that can occur within this relationship.[16]

Resistance

Resistance is not an uncommon initial response when influence is exerted upon another. The seasoned pastor is all too familiar with the cold water committee whose job it is to pour cold water on any new idea. However, it might be of some comfort to know that an initial, "No" to an idea is not necessarily a permanent, "No." When moving through change, it is important to understand that, "No" is normal. (Notice that the first two letters in the word normal are "n-o.") This resistance works both with the leader's influence upon the follower and the follower's influence upon the leader.

One of the most unproductive conclusions that can be drawn from resistance is to make such resistance a sign of spiritual immaturity, or even worse, begin believing that those who resist are of the devil. Pastors often bemoan the fact that their people are not spiritually mature and do not have enough faith to step out and believe. Similarly, members sometimes bemoan the fact that their pastor will not step out in faith and support the ministry they want to implement. Such drawing of assumptions only serves to create unspoken barriers between the two groups that taint further conversations and lead to further discord and doubt and lost productivity.

Although playing the spiritual maturity card may be initially unproductive, I need to quickly add that a lack of spiritual maturity may actually be what is hindering the church from being productive. My advice would be not to jump to the conclusion of spiritual immaturity, but to observe actions overtime. Is there eventual movement in a direction or does the status quo[17] prevail? Are people willing to continue in dialogue or are they content just to let the idea die a natural death through neglect?

If there is movement in the conversation, then it may be that people simply need more time to digest the idea. If there is no movement and no continued dialogue, then it may very well be that those whom you are attempting to influence do not have the spiritual maturity necessary to act on the idea. If this is the case, then it is the influencer's responsibility to love these persons, whether follower or leader, and seek to help them build a more intimate relationship with the Lord Jesus. As people know and understand the love of Christ, they are moved to action. The Apostle Paul said, "...it is the love of Christ that compels us" (2 Corinthians 5:14). It is not our love for Christ, but rather, an understanding of the overwhelming love of Christ for us that moves us and motivates us. Growing a person's understanding of the existence and attributes of God and the love and character of the Son is the greatest motivator.

Compliance

Compliance appears to be the prevalent response in most follower-leader relationships. Follower compliance may be defined as perfunctory obedience to the request of another but only because of the leader's legitimate position of authority. When a leader is compliant to the followers, such a response may be due to the fact that the followers hold certain amounts of influence or power over the leader. At best, compliance is activity without the whole heart. It is a pseudo-commitment that often covers itself with the trappings of loyalty and obedience, but in reality is full of guile.

Pastors and church leaders are often too willing to accept compliance as an affirmation of actions and a vote of confidence to proceed full speed to the next project. Just because the people are agreeing to act does not necessarily mean they have a full commitment toward a project. Do not be fooled into thinking that just because the members are doing what they have been requested to do and the ministry is working just fine that the church is actually functioning as a unit.

Be forewarned. Compliant responses, over time, carry the seeds of disillusionment and possible rebellion.[18] Compliant activity is an indicator that some type of coercive power may be impacting the people. There is no joy in compliance; there is only duty and legalistic adherence to a perceived requirement. The wise leader or follower needs to investigate the true motives of the people to determine why compliance is the predominant response and then teach them the freedom that comes from knowing how to follow the Lord Jesus Christ with a whole heart.

Commitment (Obedience)

Commitment is the response of faith, hope, and love. Commitment requires the whole heart. Jesus outlined our commitment to God and to our neighbor when in Mark 12: 29-31 He said,

> The first of all the commandments is: 'Hear, O Israel, the LORD our God, the LORD is one. And you shall love the LORD your God with all your heart, with all your soul, with all your mind, and with all your strength.' This is the first commandment. And the second, like it, is this: 'You shall love your neighbor as yourself.' There is no other commandment greater than these."

With an intimate commitment to God and Christ, the follower is able to trust God through the direction of a God given leader, and the leader is able to trust God to do His work through God given followers. Commitment is a response that is not so much directed at the leader or the follower but at Christ, the Head of the Church.

When leaders trust and are committed to their followers, followers are free to act more courageously, take on more responsibilities, and add to the vision and productivity of the ministry. When followers trust and are committed to their leaders, they can make the leader's leading a joy which embeds a culture of celebration within the church. There is no bickering, fighting, or positioning for power. There is a mutual commitment to follow Christ, and this mutual commitment results in a church that is spiritually empowered to accomplish the will of God. All of this unity and productivity is predicated upon each person's commitment to follow Christ first.

Commitment requires integrity.

The trustworthiness of both follower and leader can be established by each being persons of godly integrity. We need to find our wholeness in Christ and then live out the life of Christ in every detail of life. Integrity has been defined as who you are in the dark when no body sees you. This is a good definition. Followers of Christ must maintain their integrity even though those around them may not. This requires the follower of Christ to respond differently than what may be commonly expected. Consider what Paul said in Romans 12:17-21:

> Repay no one evil for evil. Have regard for good things in the sight of all men. If it is possible, as much as depends on you, live peaceably with all men. Beloved, do not avenge yourselves, but rather give place to wrath; for it is written, "Vengeance is Mine, I will repay," says the Lord. Therefore "If your enemy is hungry, feed him; If he is thirsty, give him a drink; For in so doing you will heap coals of fire on his head." Do not be overcome by evil, but overcome evil with good.

"Repay no one evil for evil...live peaceably with all men...do not avenge yourselves...overcome evil with good." How strange a place the world would be if the followers of Christ actually practiced such admonitions. How wonderful a place the church would be if the followers of Christ could at least follow these guidelines toward those within the church.

Commitment requires a price.

Maintaining a good conscience within and without the church by upholding the testimony of the Lord Jesus Christ is worth any personal price that occurs as a result of obeying His commands. If we wish to follow Christ we must respond in obedience regardless of peer pressure, political correctness, or loss of position or prestige. Christ's reputation must take priority over our own. As our behaviors change, those with whom we once associated will not understand, and they may (will) speak evil of us (1 Peter 4:4). As followers of Christ we need to remember Paul's admonition in 2 Corinthians 4:7-11:

> We are hard-pressed on every side, yet not crushed; we are perplexed, but not in despair; persecuted, but not forsaken; struck down, but not destroyed — always carrying about in the body the dying of the Lord Jesus, that the life of Jesus also may be manifested in our body. For we who live are always delivered to death for Jesus' sake, that the life of Jesus also may be manifested in our mortal flesh.

Such a following would, however, come at a personal price. Practicing such actions will cause some to call you foolish. Others will take advantage, but what of it for the sake of the glory of Christ? Any price we pay for following the Lord pales in significance to that which has already been paid by the Lord Jesus.

Commitment requires faithfulness.

One of the key characteristics of committed followers of Christ is faithfulness. All followers of Christ, whether in positions of following or leading, have been given a stewardship of the gospel of Christ and it is required of stewards that they remain faithful (1 Corinthians 4:1-2). As we have already mentioned, those followers in positions of leading are responsible for carrying out their biblical responsibilities of teaching, caring, and equipping, and those followers in positions of following are responsible for honoring, respecting, and being obedient to these leaders. For each area, faithfulness is not so much directed toward people as it is directed toward the Savior. He is our ultimate Head and we all follow Him faithfully by carrying out our assigned responsibilities within the Body of Christ.

Commitment requires humility.

Like Christ, the commitment about which I am speaking is a commitment to the will of another, God the Father. The hallmark of the follower of Christ is his or her humility to Christ and to others. In Philippians Chapter 2, Paul outlines the mind of Christ with regard to His own humility. Paul instructs us that once Christ was found in appearance as a man, He humbled Himself by becoming obedient to the point of death, even death on the cross. The essence of living a life of humility is to commit oneself to the will of another – willingly and not under compulsion. This humility usually manifests itself through a total dependence upon Christ and His Holy Spirit. When we deny self we can embrace the will of God and respond obediently to the events that surround us. In fact, not only can we respond but, in the power of the Holy Spirit, we have the opportunity to initiate actions that bring glory to God.

The Power of Submission

"You've got to be kidding!" is the usual response I get when I tell people that the most powerful action a person can take is to submit. In today's leadership circles, submission is not considered a power. The prevailing thought seems to be that leaders do not submit; leaders get others to submit to them (or as we like to say, agree to the leader's vision and plan). However, from a biblical perspective, although it appears to be paradoxical and counter-intuitive, submission is *the* way by which the follower of Christ glorifies God and influences others. I am thoroughly convinced that Scripture supports this claim. First, consider how often the Scriptures speak of submitting to God. Second, consider how often the Scriptures address submitting to one another.[19] Submission is so prevalent throughout the Scripture it appears to be the very vehicle by which the will of God is carried out in the world. To consider submission as an occasional action on the part of the follower of Christ, rather than to understand it as the constant attitude of the faithful follower in every event, is to short-circuit the power of the believer to act in the power of the Holy Spirit.

Consider the life of Jesus. As previously stated, Jesus' purpose on earth was to do the will of the Father. His life was a constant example of submission to the will of the Father. His cry in the garden of Gethsemane, "...not my will but Thine be done" (Luke 22:42) resonates in the heart of every true follower. There was no greater act of submission in the life of Christ than His submitting to death on the cross. By being the greatest follower of the will of God, Jesus became the greatest influencer (leader) of all mankind.

Speakers on leadership are fond of quoting a Chinese proverb that says something to the effect, "He who thinks he leads and turning around finds no one following, is only taking a walk." Although on the face of it such a statement would appear to be true, in reality, this Chinese philosopher never knew Jesus.

When I quote this proverb in class there is usually muffled laughter. However, when I ask the class how many of Jesus' disciples walked with Jesus on the Via Dolorosa, the way of suffering, when Christ carried His cross to His death, the laughter quickly turns to

129

soberness. The obvious answer is… no one. Not one of Jesus' closest followers followed Him to the cross. Despite all their grand statements to the contrary, when it was the will of God to die, not one follower followed. The point can be made that it was not the will of God that any of the disciples die but only Christ, for He alone was the substitutionary atoning sacrifice. Also, it fulfilled prophecy that none of Jesus' disciples joined Him in death at that time. However, such an understanding of the purpose of God was only revealed after the resurrection.

What needs to be noted is that, as the perfect follower, when Jesus was carrying His cross to Calvary, if He had looked around, He would have seen *no one* following. Yet, I doubt there are but a few who would say that Jesus was not the greatest influencer of mankind who has ever lived. Jesus was the greatest leader who ever lived and at His greatest influential moment, He had no followers. Of course there was Mary, the mother of Jesus and the other women, as well as John and quite possibly other disciples standing as observers, but observing is quite different from actively following. The lesson for all followers is this: Jesus influenced the world by walking *alone* in the will of God.

According to some leadership teaching, the ministry of Jesus would be an abject failure. From the prevailing leadership perspective that numerical increase is indicative of ministry success, an assessment of the ministry of the preacher from Galilee might include the following questions: How is it that the greatest leader who ever lived did not have the leader capacity to rally his followers around him at this moment of crisis? Did Jesus fail to be a transformational leader at certain times in the disciples' development? Did Jesus miss an aspect of situational leadership theory where He coached when he should have directed? Perhaps Jesus should have been more of a servant leader to His disciples. Sounds ridiculous doesn't it?

Of course, none of these questions are relevant. These questions represent the rationalizations we create when we try and explain the failures of our contemporaries. When a church does not grow or a ministry fails we think, "Surely, there was a leadership flaw somewhere." Yet, to attribute a flaw to Christ, especially at the most important moment of his earthly existence is unacceptable. There has to be another reason.

It is apparent from the Scriptures that Jesus' submission to the will of the Father required Him to follow a path of sacrifice that His followers, at least at that moment, were unwilling to follow. Is it possible that Jesus' example at this moment of His life can give us some insight into what perfectly following the will of God might mean to us as followers of Christ? Consider the following points:

1. As a leader (influencer) of others, submission to the will of God may require us to follow His will *alone*. This act of obedience does not void a leader's influence.
2. The absence of the physical presence of followers does not mean you are not leading (influencing). If leading others is predicated upon the actual presence of followers, then we may be tempted not to follow the will of God if it will cost us our following.
3. One never knows how the Holy Spirit will use a lone act of obedience to influence the lives of observers or even those who might hear of such obedience. One need only look at the lives of the martyrs to gain a greater appreciation for the influence that results from following the will of God. Such following does not necessarily have to result in physical death to have significant influence.
4. Self-preservation is the biggest detriment to submitting to the will of God. I have observed among leaders that self-preservation largely revolves around one's ego and the desire to protect one's reputation at all costs.

If we continue to teach that great leaders are defined by the numbers of their followers, those in positions of influence may never understand that it is through submission to the will of God, regardless of the consequences, that ultimately brings about the greatest influence in the lives of others to the glory of God. Through submission we point the focus of everyone's attention away from ourselves as a leader to Christ before whom we are submitting. This submission to Christ is one basis Paul taught in Philippians 3:17-19 when choosing whom to follow:

131

Brethren, join in following my example, and note those who so walk, as you have us for a pattern. For many walk, of whom I have told you often, and now tell you even weeping, that they are the enemies of the cross of Christ: whose end is destruction, whose god is their belly, and whose glory is in their shame — who set their mind on earthly things.

The word, "following" in this verse is the Greek word from which we get our English word "imitate".[20] Paul was fond of this particular descriptor and used it to encourage believers in their devotion to Christ.[21] The use of this word is significant in that submission to the Lord is not only an attribute in the heart of the follower, but is manifested through actions. Submissive followers, who serve as organizational leaders, walk according to a particular biblical pattern. Looking at the context of Philippians we can readily see that this pattern was evidenced in the life of Paul (Philippians 3: 4-16), Epaphroditus (Philippians 3:25-30), Timothy (Philippians 3:19-24), and Jesus Christ (Philippians 2:1-11). The biblical pattern we are to imitate is an undiluted devotion to God and Christ and His commands.[22]

As a practical matter, submission effectively influences people toward you and your position. Surveys indicate that humility, honesty, and integrity are personal characteristics that influence others to want to follow.[23] Each one of these characteristics is a byproduct of submission. Humility is a byproduct of a willingness to accept others as better than yourself (Philippians 2:3). Honesty is a byproduct of submitting to the standards of do not lie, do not steal, do not bear false witness (Romans 13:9-10). Integrity is a byproduct of being made whole through a relationship with Christ and following His commandments (John 17:21). People follow those who act submissively.

An illustration you might try in order to show how follower submission can move a leader in your direction is to designate yourself as the follower. Then, have a person stand facing you designated as the leader. Next, have the person hold their hands over their head, palms facing toward you. You take the same position and put your palms together. Slowly, each of you move your feet backward until the weight is evenly distributed between you, forming an arch, and are both dependent on each other to keep from falling flat on your faces. At that moment, as the follower, release the pressure by pulling your arms toward you and the other person will take a step toward you. They will have to take a step forward or fall flat. I use this illustration in class as a way of showing that acts of submission, not power and control, are the crucial influence in an interdependent relationship. The same illustration can be used to show how leader submission can move followers in their direction as well. What is clear from the Scriptures is that an attitude of submission to Christ and the Bible needs to permeate the follower-leader relationships within the church. The Holy Spirit enables us to be submissive. Others may take advantage of us on occasion. This is to be expected. However, even then, as we submit ourselves to God's Word and live submitted to the power of God's Holy Spirit, our actions will ultimately redound to the Glory of God.

The Enabling of the Holy Spirit

I love the word enable. Embedded in this word is the idea of dependence upon something (or someone) before any other activity can take place. The word depicts the position of every follower of Christ as being totally dependent upon God for everything. A life without the enabling power of the Holy Spirit can only accomplish what human effort can produce.

Asking God to help in time of need is a beautiful expression of our dependence upon Him. Unfortunately, the idea of asking God for help has the potential of mutating into a works-oriented, unbiblical idea of God doing His part and me doing my part, as if I could do something on my own and in my own strength to aid God in accomplishing His will. What needs to be in the forefront of the follower's mind is an absolute dependence on God. For me to do any part in accomplishing God's will requires that I be enabled by His Spirit to act. What actions, gifts, and abilities I employ in obeying Christ's commands are gifts that He has given.[24]

I am concerned that our concentration on leader styles, leader characteristics, and leader behaviors has subtly diminished a dependence on the Holy Spirit. Rather than depending upon the Holy Spirit, we may subconsciously be tempted to rely upon the cleverly devised philosophies of men. Followers of Christ must resist such temptations and constantly rely upon nothing and no one but the Holy Spirit to influence. Failing to recognize our need leads to pride and reliance upon human ability to create change rather than giving all glory to God. Such self-aggrandizement eventually results in nothing short of idolatry.

J. Oswald Sanders wrote, "Spiritual leadership requires Spirit-filled people. Other qualities are important; to be Spirit-filled is indispensable,"[25] Sanders completed his thoughts regarding this essential element of submission by writing:

> To be filled with the Spirit means simply that the Christian voluntarily surrenders life and will to the Spirit. Through faith, the believer's personality is filled, mastered, and controlled by the Spirit. The meaning of "filled" is not "to pour into a passive container" but to "take possession of the mind." That's the meaning found in Luke 5:26: "They were filled with awe." When we invite the Spirit to fill us, the Spirit's power grips our lives with this kind of strength and passion.
>
> To be filled with the Spirit is to be controlled by the Spirit. The Christian leader's mind, emotions, will, and physical strength all become available for the Spirit to guide and use. Under the Spirit's control, natural gifts of leadership are lifted to their highest power, sanctified for holy purpose. Through the work of the now ungrieved and unhindered Spirit, all the fruits of the Spirit start to grow in the leader's life. His witness is more winsome, service more steady, and testimony more powerful. All real Christian service is but the expression of the Spirit's power through believers yielded to Him (John 7:71-39).[26]

Conclusion

I hope you have been able to see that followers of Christ have influence whether they are identified as leaders or followers. There is never a time when we are not influencing others. This is why it is crucial that everyone in the church knows and understands his or her biblical follower responsibilities. The interdependent relationships that are the basis of decision making within the church depend upon followers of Christ who are filled with His Spirit, submissive to the will of God, responsive to His commands, and sensitive to those around them.

Those identified as leaders must also understand that being a Follower First may require them to make difficult decisions that at times may result in many followers, if not all, refusing to follow. At these times, the Follower First leader is called to persevere and trust the promises of God. Additionally, the Follower First leader understands that influencing others does not always happen openly or immediately. God's timetable is often much longer than ours. However, through a heart submitted to God and actions to match, the faithful follower can be used of God to influence many.

135

The Follower's Influence

Authority and Power
- Societal Constructs
  - Governments
  - Bondservants and Masters
  - Parents
  - Elders

Pastoral Authority

Types of Power
- Reward
- Coercive
- Expert
- Referent
- Structural
- Resource
- Information

Quid Pro Quo

Responses
- Resistance
- Compliance
- Commitment

The Power of Submission

The Enabling of the Holy Spirit

Chapter 6

Following-Leaders: The Exercise of Influence

Those who embrace the Follower First philosophy are not dependent on titles or positions in order to gain a sense of identity and worth. They understand that good leaders *are* good followers. They realize that being a faithful follower of Christ enables them to influence everyone with whom they have contact. This influence is not based upon status or rank within the organization. It comes as a natural byproduct of being a Follower First. Those who are Followers First are committed to Christ, not a cause or an organization. Those who make up the church should only follow leaders who follow Christ. In other words, the church is to be led by Following-Leaders.

With all the other leadership styles and theories available, I submit that the Following-Leader is the primary leader style for the church's unique organizational structure and purpose. At first glance, the idea of a Following-Leader appears to be oxymoronic. How can a person be following and leading at the same time in the same position? The answer to the question lies in understanding the definitions of following and leading.

Following Defined

The Follower First philosophy defines following as willingly following the Lord Jesus Christ with all one's heart, mind, soul, and strength in every circumstance regardless of organizational position. The follower may or may not have a recognized position of responsibility in the organization. However, one's position does not determine the passion and integrity of the Follower First follower. First, these followers understand their primary submission is to the Lord and His commands. Second, the follower willingly submits to those whom the Lord has given oversight for them as long as these leaders are fellow followers of Christ. Third, the follower willingly submits to every human institution in order to give a good testimony to those who do not follow Christ. Followers are who they are, and following the Lord is what they do.

Leading Defined

Leaders may be defined as those whom followers follow. More precisely, leaders are the persons in most definitions of leadership who exercise influence. Peter Northouse defines leadership as "a process whereby an individual influences a group of individuals to achieve a common goal."[1]

The ability to influence appears to be a primary function of what it means to be a leader. Although there are certainly other aspects, this ability to influence is a key element of leading others. It may also be said that anyone exercising influence over another person could be understood as leading others whether this person holds a recognized position of leadership within the organization or not. Thus, with this understanding, biblical followers may be considered Following-Leaders. Perhaps a more apt, but bulky, description is to call them following-influencers.

As we have mentioned, Joseph Rost, Ira Chaleff, and others recognize that the follower-leader relationship is not based upon a cause-effect linear relationship in which the leader acts and the follower responds. We have already seen that the interdependence between leader and follower is much too complicated to rely upon the idea that "everything rises or falls on leadership." Chaleff suggests that leaders and followers revolve around a common purpose in the organization. Within a church context, the follower and leader revolve around a person, the Lord Jesus Christ (See Figure 6). It is this interplay between a designated leader and a follower that allows the leader to follow at certain times within certain contexts and the follower to lead at certain times in certain contexts. The Follower First philosophy is unique in that throughout the leader-follower relationship the idea is never lost that both leader and follower are always following the Lord Jesus. We can see this same relationship illustrated through the Mobius Strip in Chapter 3.

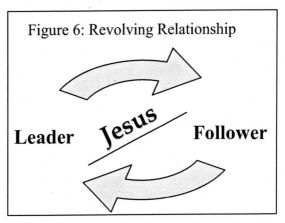

Figure 6: Revolving Relationship

Leader *Jesus* Follower

Being a Follower

Recalling the diagram from Chapter One, one can see that followers always consider themselves followers (see Figure 7). When followers assume responsibility over others, the follower is often called a leader. Thus, wherever followers are within an organizational hierarchy, whether the custodian or the president, the Follower First philosophy requires the follower to assess himself or herself as a Follower First. One of the unique aspects of being a Following-Leader is that those who embrace the Follower First philosophy only need be who they are within the organization and, by default, they become Following-Leaders. That is, there is no need to concentrate on *becoming* something other than who they already are. By being followers of Christ where they are within the organization, with a leader title or without, the followers' actions and responses influence those around them. They are being Following-Leaders.

Figure 7: A Following-Leader is Born

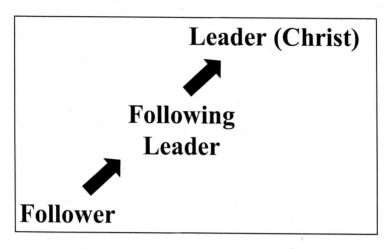

The influence of the Following-Leader increases when he or she is given responsibility over others within the organization. As a follower with a title, the follower has the opportunity to influence and to lead, others in a way that glorifies God. However, it bears repeating that one of the subtle temptations within organizations is for followers to begin thinking of themselves as leaders first rather than followers first. The Following-Leader construct can be a corrective way of thinking for the leader and an accurate way for followers to think about their leaders.

A Way of Thinking for Leaders

One way of defining success in life is finding what God wants you to do and accomplishing it in the power of the Holy Spirit. If I could add anything to this definition I think I would add that success in life is finding what God wants me to Be and Being that person in the power of the Holy Spirit. The reason I make the change is because, if I am the person I am called by God to be, then I naturally will do the things I am commanded by God to do. It is through a submissive relationship to the Savior that I find fulfillment.

My relationship to Christ became clearer to me when on a hunting trip I was confronted by the question, "What is eternal life?" As I thought about the answer, I worked through the simple definitions. Eternal life is life eternal, or as the young people at church might retort, eternal life is living forever. Some might think that heaven is eternal life, but heaven is actually the place where we live out eternal life. Then I stumbled upon John 17:3 where Jesus actually defines eternal life:

> "And this is eternal life, that they might know Thee, the only true God, and Jesus Christ whom Thou hast sent."

According to Jesus, eternal life is knowing God and Jesus Christ. Leave it to the Savior to give such a precise definition. However, I was then confronted with the question, "How do I know God and Jesus Christ?"

I gain eternal life when I intimately know God through a relationship with Jesus Christ. I increase my intimate knowledge of Jesus as He reveals Himself to me as I follow His commands. I experience eternal life daily as I become the person He wants me to be and recognize every event of every day as an opportunity to revel in my personal relationship with God through Jesus Christ. When God provides an opportunity for the follower to lead, He is opening an opportunity for the leader to know Jesus more intimately. The position does entail more responsibility over others. However, let us never forget that the purpose of the follower of Christ being in a leader position is so that God can honor Himself through the Following-Leader, and so that the Following-Leader can experience eternal life through greater dependence upon Jesus.

Dependence is gained through obedience to the commands of Jesus. Jesus said in John 14:21, "He who has My commandments and keeps them, it is he who loves Me. And he who loves Me will be loved by My Father, and I will love him and manifest Myself to him." As the believer becomes more and more dependent upon Christ through obeying His commands, Jesus promises to reveal (manifest) himself to the believer. Thus, the one who follows the commands of Jesus becomes a follower who has an intimate relationship with God and with Jesus. Through this intimacy a greater love for God is created which begins a process of falling more in love with Jesus, which produces greater obedience to His word, which allows Jesus to reveal more of Himself to the follower, which creates a greater love for God, which produces a greater love for Jesus, which produces greater obedience, etc. This process continues as long as the follower is obedient to the commands of Christ or until the follower dies and goes to be with the Lord in heaven.

Why is it important to understand this process? If we think that leading others is just an exercise in being successful, or being the best me I can be, or fulfilling my destiny, or growing an organization, or making an impact, or doing what others cannot do, then we miss the very point of being a Following-Leader. We are robbed of the very purpose for living out our eternal life on this earth. If I do not know the purpose behind being a follower and a leader, then all the success in the world goes for naught. However, if I think correctly about who I am and that God has me in the positions in which I function in this life so that I might know Him in all His fullness, then life, and struggle, and hurt, and pain, and joy, and relationships take on an entirely deeper meaning, and I experience "life, and that abundantly" (John 10:10). Following and leading are ultimately *not* about following a leader or leading others. **Following a leader and leading others are about knowing God.**

A Way for Followers to Think About Their Leaders

If leading others is about knowing God, then why follow? Following is about knowing God from a different perspective. When we find ourselves in an organization and there are leaders placed over us, our first concern is to determine if the leader is a Following-Leader. One way to determine this is to ask the leader what or who he or she is following. The answer will reveal whether the person is someone who understands that he/she is a follower of Christ first and whether or not this is the person under whom you can serve.

As a follower, I am not looking for a perfect leader. I already have one in the person of Christ. My desire is to honor God and obey the Lord's commands by supporting my human leader as much as I am able. As long as the leader is leading me into intimacy with the Savior, I can support the leader. However, if the time comes when the leader acts in immoral or unbiblical ways, I am required to confront the leader, gently correct him/her, and if there is no change, remove myself and my family from the influence of this leader who is no longer, by definition, a Following-Leader.

One thing that needs to be kept in mind is that followers of Christ who do not hold positions within an organization can still be effective Following-Leaders. The fact that you do not hold a title or position does not prohibit you from acting consistently with the Scriptures in your daily activities and influencing (leading) those around you to greater obedience to the commands of the Lord. In fact, Following-Leaders influence others wherever they are.

When the current leadership literature offers guidance on identifying potential leaders, what these authors are really identifying are the characteristics of Following-Leaders. One writer suggests looking for the following characteristics when looking to recruit leaders:

Character	Evident Gifts
Influence	Proven Track Record
Positive Attitude	Confidence
People Skills	Self-Discipline
Communication Skills	Discontent with *Status Quo*[2]

Do any of these traits look familiar? They do because they are the very same characteristics of a person who lives his or her life with a Follower First philosophy. What the leadership literature does not admit is that when leaders are looking for people to serve with them, they are not *really* looking for leaders but followers who have consistently lived out the Follower First philosophy. Think about it. How does anyone get recognized for additional responsibility? They fulfill the requests of others in ways that evidence integrity, competence, and humility. They exhibit the characteristics of a person who knows who he or she is and acts according to core values that are congruent with the organization. Leaders don't need more leaders. There can only be so many chefs in the kitchen. Leaders are really looking for Following-Leaders.

If, as a follower of the Person and teachings of Jesus Christ, I am already a Following-Leader, how might I become a more committed follower and more effective influencer of others? As I understand it, this is a lifelong process of denying self, taking up my cross daily, and following the Lord. The following are some practical applications of how that process may be completed. These applications are not intended to be comprehensive or prescriptive, but merely suggestions from my own journey as a follower.

1. Love the Perfect Follower

As a believer, the primary benefit for leading others is coming to know more intimately the perfect follower, the Lord Jesus Christ. This requires the Following-Leader to spend more time with the Lord in prayer and study of the Bible. This requirement is crucial in the future readiness of the Following-Leader to lead others, especially when the will of God begins to require personal sacrifice.

Jesus' own disciples expressed this point clearly, when after Jesus had spoken a difficult teaching, the people began to leave the ranks. Jesus asked His disciples if they too would leave. The answer was spoken by Peter in John 6:68-69, "Lord, to whom shall we go? You have the words of eternal life. Also we have come to believe and know that You are the Christ, the Son of the living God." Jesus has the words of eternal life. These are the words that are not only good for salvation from sin but for living out the abundant life of Christ on earth. Additionally, Jesus is the Christ. He is not just an ideal or a good idea. These men staked their eternal souls on the belief that Jesus was the Christ, the Messiah. According to tradition, most of Jesus' true disciples died a martyrs' death.[3]

One practical means by which the Following-Leader can grow in a relationship with Jesus is through prayer. There are many good books regarding prayer, but one in particular is Andrew Murrays' classic, *With Christ in the School of Prayer*. Murray wrote:

> The place and power of prayer in the Christian life is too little understood. As long as we view prayer simply as the means of maintaining our own Christian lives, we will not fully understand what it is really supposed to be. But when we learn to regard it as the highest part of the work entrusted to us – the root and

strength of all other work - we will see that there is nothing we need to study and practice more than the art of praying.[4]

2. Apply God's Word

The Bible is the Following-Leader's major textbook for understanding how to act and respond in life situations. He/she must thirst for the Word. Deep within the follower there must be a need to hear from God through the Word of God. As an example to others, the Following-Leader applies teachings from the Word which others may call foolish or naïve. Even though the world system may play by a different set of rules, the Following-Leader refuses to compromise and is willing to be defrauded rather than besmirch the character and reputation of Christ. Without question, this application of the Word in life, business, and family may result in being taken advantage of by others. Still, obedience to the Word of God is paramount in maintaining that which is primary to the Following-Leader, a continuing intimacy with the Lord Jesus Christ.

For Following-Leaders, the Bible establishes both their ethic and worldview. The Bible determines their core values which in turn affect how they make decisions, the direction and goals for their life and ministry, how to resolve conflicts, as well as set priorities for themselves and the ministry.[5] Knowing the Bible and applying its teachings to life is the daily practice of the Following-Leader.

3. Love and Seek to Understand People

One of the sweetest expressions of care in the New Testament is seen when Paul sends Timothy to the church at Philippi because "I have no one else of kindred spirit who will genuinely be concerned for your welfare. For they all seek after their own interests, not those of Christ Jesus" (Philippians 2:20-21). Paul often shared his heart of love and concern with the churches. Consider Paul's words when He wrote the Thessalonians in 1 Thessalonians 2:1-12:

But we were gentle among you, just as a nursing mother cherishes her own children. So, affectionately longing for you, we were well pleased to impart to you not only the gospel of God, but also our own lives, because you had become dear to us. For you remember, brethren, our labor and toil; for laboring night and day, that we might not be a burden to any of you, we preached to you the gospel of God. You are witnesses, and God also, how devoutly and justly and blamelessly we behaved ourselves among you who believe; as you know how we exhorted, and comforted, and charged every one of you, as a father does his own children, that you would walk worthy of God who calls you into His own kingdom and glory.

Even though he has spiritual authority as an apostle, Paul's self-perception is not as a supervisor, leader, or authority figure, but as a nursing mother and a caring father. Paul understood that the church, with all her faults, is still the Bride of Christ who must be cherished and nurtured.

Paul could write these words because of his deep understanding of the love of Christ (2 Corinthians 5:14). Paul had been a recipient of the compassion and love of Christ, a gift which he never forgot or took for granted. Following-Leaders emulate this same type of compassion for others.

In Matthew 9:35-38 when Jesus saw the people as sheep without a shepherd, Matthew shares that Jesus was "moved with compassion."

Then Jesus went about all the cities and villages, teaching in their synagogues, preaching the gospel of the kingdom, and healing every sickness and every disease among the people. But when He saw the multitudes, He was moved with compassion for them, because they were weary and scattered, like sheep having no shepherd. Then He said to His disciples, "The harvest truly is plentiful, but the laborers are few. Therefore pray the Lord of the harvest to send out laborers into His harvest."

The word "compassion" can be literally translated "moved in the bowels."[6] Put in everyday language; the word compassion conveys the idea that when Jesus saw the plight of the multitude, such an emotional experience literally made His stomach hurt. If we are to follow Jesus, we, too must demonstrate similar compassion.

Following-Leaders realize that everyone in the church is broken in some way. God has populated His church with persons the world system designates as losers. Consider what Paul says in 1 Corinthians 1:26-31:

> For you see your calling, brethren, that not many wise according to the flesh, not many mighty, not many noble, are called. But God has chosen the foolish things of the world to put to shame the wise, and God has chosen the weak things of the world to put to shame the things which are mighty; and the base things of the world and the things which are despised God has chosen, and the things which are not, to bring to nothing the things that are, that no flesh should glory in His presence. But of Him you are in Christ Jesus, who became for us wisdom from God — and righteousness and sanctification and redemption — that, as it is written, "He who glories, let him glory in the LORD."

Jesus points out in Luke 14:21 that it is "the poor, and the maimed, and the lame and the blind" who will be invited to the banquet table of His blessing. All of us who populate the church fall into this category. We are nothing special in ourselves. God has extended His grace toward us and we must never forget from where we came. Additionally, if we would lead a church of the foolish and the weak, does it not follow that the leaders would be the weakest and the most foolish of all?

4. Develop Integrity

The most highly prized values that researchers contend are essential to good leaders are clearly taught in the Scriptures.[7] Some of these values are:

147

(a) Honesty - "You shall have honest scales, honest weights" (Leviticus 19:36).

(b) Integrity - "The integrity of the upright will guide them but the perversity of the unfaithful will destroy them" (Proverbs: 11:3).

(c) Justice - "You shall do no injustice in judgment. You shall not be partial to the poor nor honor the person of the mighty. In righteousness you shall judge your neighbor" (Leviticus 19:15).

(d) Humility - "Humble yourself in the eyes of the Lord, and He will lift you up" (James 4:10).

Following-Leaders need to examine their personal beliefs and values to determine the basis for their decision making. Moving away from biblical core values may be subtly incremental. However, over time these subtle actions are extremely detrimental to achieving the overall purpose of the church.

The essence of the word integrity is wholeness. As followers of Christ, we are complete in Him (Colossians 2:10). However, if we allow compromise to enter our decision making process at the level of our core values, we run the risk of losing our influence in the lives of others. The essence of the Following-Leader's personal integrity is pleasing God in all we say and do. 1 Thessalonians 2:1-6 outlines Paul's personal integrity:

> For you yourselves know, brethren, that our coming to you was not in vain. But even after we had suffered before and were spitefully treated at Philippi, as you know, we were bold in our God to speak to you the gospel of God in much conflict. For our exhortation did not come from error or uncleanness, nor was it in deceit. But as we have been approved by God to be entrusted with the gospel, even so we speak, not as pleasing men, but God who tests our hearts. For neither at any time did we use flattering words, as you know, nor a cloak for covetousness — God is witness. Nor did we seek glory from men, either from you or from others, when we might have made demands as apostles of Christ.

The Following-Leader speaks, "...not as pleasing men, but God who tests our hearts." Being sensitive to the promptings of the Holy Spirit, the Following-Leader speaks the truths of the Bible even when unpopular with the hearers. This does not mean there will never be a time when the Following-Leader misspeaks. However, being sensitive to the Holy Spirit, the Following-Leader will humble himself or herself before others and make the needed correction so that truth might prevail.

5. Develop Avenues of Influence

The primary desire of the Following-Leader is following the will of the Lord and is evidenced through many different leader styles. Certain leadership theories lend themselves well to the Following-Leader philosophy. Space will not permit a full explanation of these theories. However, below is a brief overview of some of the more pertinent leadership theories and styles that are congruent with a Follower First philosophy:

Leader-Member Exchange

The Leader-Member Exchange theory (LMX)[8] focuses on the interactions between leaders and followers. It is "the only leadership approach that makes the concept of the dyadic relationship the centerpiece of leadership process."[9] The theory posits that within organizations leaders build relationships with *in-group* persons (those who take on greater responsibilities and build relationship with the leader) and with *out-group* persons (those content with a more formal, job description-driven relationship to the leader). These relationships are built upon an exchange where the leader does more for those followers who are in the in-group than those who, because of their lack of involvement in the leader-follower relationship, become the out-group.

It is not uncommon for persons to consider certain aspects of the Courageous Follower and Exemplary Follower theories to be expressions of the LMX Theory. At first glance, such a comparison does lend itself to consider courageous followers to be those in the in-group and all other follower types to compose the out-group. However, such an observation fails to consider that the LMX theory considers the activities of the leader toward the follower as the one building the relationship rather than the follower initiating the relationship and supporting the leader. This distinction is important when considering the LMX theory in relation to the Follower First Philosophy.

The Follower First Philosophy perceives the in-group relationship as one that the follower is responsible to build rather than depending and waiting on the initiation of the leader. The follower understands his/her role as being the one who moves close to the leader and seeks to meet the leader's needs.

Additionally, the Follower First follower understands that the quality of the relationship between the follower and the leader is not built upon a desire for exchanges offered by the leader. These potential benefits offered by the leader to the follower are inconsequential as the biblical follower seeks to fulfill his/her duty to the leader. The basis for the relationship is not built upon what the follower can *get* from the relationship as much as what the follower can *give* to the relationship. This attitude of an "unprofitable servant" (Luke 17:10) carries over into all aspects of the follower's role and responsibility within the organization.

Charismatic Leadership

Although not used in the theological sense of a person having the spiritual gift of speaking in tongues, charismatic leaders were initially defined by Max Weber[10] as those who have special personality characteristics that give a person superhuman or exceptional powers reserved for a few, are of divine origin, and result in the person being treated as a leader.[11] This view resonates with those who hold to leaders being born with certain traits that propel them into leading roles within organizations.

Robert House[12] suggested that charismatic leaders display six specific behaviors:

1. They set a strong role model for the beliefs and values they want their followers to adopt.
2. They appear competent to followers.
3. They articulate ideological goals that have moral overtones.
4. They communicate high expectations for followers.
5. They exhibit confidence in followers' abilities to meet these expectations.
6. They arouse task-relevant motives in followers that may include affiliation, power, or esteem.[13]

Those Following-Leaders who are gifted to communicate may find this ability allows them to build trust with their fellow followers as they seek to accomplish the church's goals. One aspect of this leadership style that needs to be guarded is that followers may have a tendency to become so enamored with the leader they begin to follow without question. This unquestioning acceptance may need to be diverted away from the human leader and toward the person of Jesus Christ. Additionally, the charismatic leader is prone to begin seeking power through other people rather than following the Lord Jesus. This *gift* then becomes the cause for many being led astray from an intimate relationship with the Lord in exchange for a temporary relationship with the leader.

Transformational Leadership

Introduced in 1978 by James MacGregor Burns,[14] the transformational leadership theory sought to link the role of leaders and followers. Transformational leadership may be defined as,

> a process whereby a person engages with others and creates a connection that raises the level of motivation and morality in both the leader and the follower. This type of leader is attentive

to the needs and motives of followers and tries to help followers reach their fullest potential.[15]

Bernard Bass[16] extended the work of Burns by arguing there are four distinct factors involved in the transformational leadership process:

1. **Idealized Influence**
   It describes leaders who act as strong role models for followers; followers identify with these leaders and want very much to emulate them. These leaders usually have very high standards of moral and ethical conduct and can be counted on to do the right thing. They are deeply respected by followers, who usually place a great deal of trust in them. They provide followers with a vision and a sense of mission.[17]

2. **Inspirational Motivation**
   This factor is descriptive of leaders who communicate high expectations to followers, inspiring them through motivation to become committed to and part of the shared vision in the organization. In practice, leaders use symbols and emotional appeals to focus group members' efforts to achieve more than they would in their own self-interest.[18]

3. **Intellectual Stimulation**
   It includes leadership that stimulates followers to be creative and innovative and to challenge their own beliefs and values as well as those of the leader and the organization. This type of leadership supports followers as they try new approaches and develop innovative ways of dealing with organizational issues. It encourages followers to think things out on their own and engage in careful problem solving.[19]

4. **Individualized Consideration**
   This factor is representative of leaders who provide a supportive climate in which they listen carefully to the individual needs of followers. Leaders act as coaches and advisers while trying to assist followers in becoming fully actualized. These leaders may use delegation to help followers grow through personal challenges.[20]

The Following-Leader may take on the characteristics of a Transformational Leader as he or she seeks to inspire his or her followers to achieve even greater things to the glory of God. The Transformational Leader style is preferred over the Transactional Leader style because Transactional leaders rely upon a negotiated exchange relationship with the follower in which the leader agrees to provide certain benefits when the follower fulfills the wishes of the leader. The Following-Leader seeks to raise the level of the leader-follower relationship to one in which both leader and follower are responding based upon a common desire to honor God. The Following-Leader also understands that it is the role and responsibility of the Holy Spirit to inspire (John 6:44; John 15:5). All appreciation or adulation from others is quickly deflected to the ultimate leader, the Lord Jesus Christ.

Servant Leadership

Introduced by Robert Greenleaf in 1977,[21] the servant leadership model has become quite popular within the church. Greenleaf developed his theory after reading Hermann Hesse's novel, *Journey to the East*, a story about a group of people on a spiritual quest. Greenleaf determined that a great leader is first experienced by others as a servant. Thus, the greatness of a leader rests with his or her willingness to serve others.

Such a concept is well received by many Christians because of Jesus' emphasizing His role as a servant when He said in Matthew 20:28, "...the Son of Man did not come to be served, but to serve, and to give His life a ransom for many." Additionally, Jesus emphasized the servant role His disciples should take when He said in Matthew 20:26, "Whoever desires to become great among you, let him be your servant."

Larry Spears, President and CEO of the Spears Center for Servant-Leadership (www.spearscenter.org), has extracted a set of ten characteristics of servant leaders:[22]

1. *Listening:*
He or she seeks to listen receptively to what is being said and not said.

2. *Empathy:*
People need to be accepted and recognized for their special and unique spirits.

3. *Healing:*
Although this is a part of being human, servant-leaders recognize that they have an opportunity to "help make whole" those with whom they come in contact.

4. *Awareness:*
General awareness, and especially self-awareness, strengthens the servant-leader.

5. *Persuasion:*
The servant-leader seeks to convince others, rather than coerce compliance.

6. *Conceptualization:*
Servant-leaders seek to nurture their abilities to "dream great dreams."

7. *Foresight:*
Foresight is a characteristic that enables the servant-leader to understand the lessons from the past, the realities of the present, and the likely consequence of a decision for the future. It is also deeply rooted within the intuitive mind deserving of careful attention.

8. *Stewardship:*
Robert Greenleaf's view of all institutions was one in which CEOs, staffs, and trustees all played significant roles in holding their institutions in trust for the greater good of society.

9. *Commitment to the growth of people:*
Servant-leaders believe that people have an intrinsic value beyond their tangible contributions as workers.

10. *Building community:*
Greenleaf said: "All that is needed to rebuild community as a viable life form for large numbers of people is for enough servant-leaders to show the way, not by mass movements, but by each servant-leader demonstrating his own unlimited liability for a quite specific community-related group."

Another scholar, Kathleen Patterson, understands servant leadership as a virtuous theory by which the servant leader's focus is follower-focused rather than primarily focused on organizational objectives. Patterson suggests that there are seven virtuous constructs present in the process of servant leadership.[23] They are:

1. Agapao – A Greek term for moral love that seeks to do the right thing at the right time.
2. Humility – The trait of keeping one's accomplishments and talents in perspective.
3. Altruism – A concern for the welfare of others.
4. Vision – The capacity to see others as worthy and seeks to assist each person in reaching that state.
5. Trust – An essential component of the follower/leader relationship built upon mutual respect and integrity.
6. Empowerment – Giving power to others.
7. Service – Giving of oneself.

Figure 8 illustrates Patterson's model by which servant leaders influence others. By leading with Agapao, the leader exhibits humility and altruism. These two constructs interact with vision and trust ultimately resulting in empowering others. The ultimate goal of this empowerment is service.

Figure 8: Patterson's Servant Leadership Model[24]

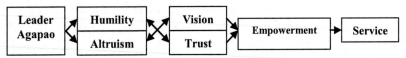

Perhaps the Follower First philosophy can best apply to servant leadership as an answer to the questions posed by Peter Senge in the afterward of Greenleaf's, *Servant Leadership*. Senge inquires:

> What does it take to cultivate a genuine desire to serve? I can't think of any more important question. What keeps us from accessing, realizing, and acting from an innate desire to serve? I do not think these questions have simple answers. But I do think they are the right questions. The answers have to be personal. They also have to be situational. But this is where the journey starts.[25]

What does it take to cultivate a genuine desire to serve? The Follower First perspective would say it takes a life made new by the Lord Jesus Christ. What keeps us from accessing, realizing, and acting from an innate desire to serve? The Bible makes it clear that our basic sinfulness, our selfish desires to be served rather than serve others, is the greatest hindrance to being true servants to others. Senge is correct. The answers do have to be personal, but they are not situational. The Follower First philosophy of Following-Leaders operates from a pan-cultural perspective. Following-Leaders are who they are regardless of the situation. Their motivation, purpose, and desire do not change from context to context. This sense of stability gives the Following-Leader the integrity he or she needs to face the challenges of influencing others, and it gives followers the consistency they need to trust and be trusted by their leaders.

Because Following-Leaders base their leading on a Follower First philosophy, they may embrace many leader styles. The leader style of the Following-Leader is contingent upon the personality, giftedness, training, and spiritual maturity of the particular Following-Leader. In one instance the Following-Leader may manifest more service orientation and in another he/she may evidence more inspiration. Following-Leaders understand that God superintends over each follower-leader context and through the Holy Spirit will enable them to perform in a style that best brings glory to God. Thus, Following-Leaders seek to concentrate on being who they are in Christ and leading from this position.

Following-Leader Responses to Following-Leaders

Following-Leaders make the best responders to other Following-Leaders who are in positions of authority. These Following-Leaders recognize that the person in authority has responsibilities and that the followers will play a crucial role in the success or failure of the one in authority. Therefore, because Following-Leaders who lead are clear with regard to whom and what they follow, it is easy for Following-Leaders who follow to respond positively to the leader. These followers take the lead in responding to the leaders and give joy to the leader. This, "How can we help?" and "How can we serve?" attitude creates an atmosphere of mutual respect and trust.

To the Charismatic Following-Leader the follower responds positively to his/her beliefs and values because the follower's values are congruent with that of the leader. Followers rally to the charismatic Following-Leader because their ideological goals and morals are shared thus creating a dynamic of mutual high expectation and confidence to meet these expectations. Follower First followers do not idolize these leaders, but they do enjoy their company because of their mutual love for and expressions of love to the Lord Jesus Christ.

To the Transformational Following-Leader, the follower responds in ways that help accentuate the leader's style. **Idealized Influence** is recognized through the modeling of the leader and because this modeling is exactly how the follower acts and responds, a positive follower response serves to reinforce the moral and ethical conduct of the leader. Open communication between follower and leader allows the vision of the follower and the vision of the leader to be respectfully shared, discussed, and implemented. The **Inspirational Motivation** of the leader is matched by the inspired motivation of the follower. Because the follower shares the high expectation of the leader, little is needed by way of symbols and emotional appeals to motivate the follower to action. The humility and selflessness of the follower often inspires the leader to greater acts of selfless leading and serving. **Intellectual Stimulation** is a reciprocal relationship. Because neither the leader nor the follower considers himself or herself to be *the* authority or expert on a matter, there is always an atmosphere of openness to new ideas and mutual encouragement to learn. Creativity by all is embraced with enthusiasm and new ways of dealing with situations are celebrated as long as they adhere to biblical teaching. Followers embrace the **Individualized Consideration** of the leader and understand that he/she has strengths and weaknesses. Follower acceptance of personality quirks and not demanding that the leader be perfect allow the leader to embrace his/her humanity and become more authentic before the followers. This, in turn, creates a greater level of trust and respect resulting in greater productivity on the part of leader and follower.

To the Servant Leader, followers readily embrace and reciprocate the desire to serve. Followers exemplify all ten of Sperry's traits and contextualize them toward the leader. Followers listen to leaders, have empathy for them and their positions, are aware of their power to make or break the leader, use persuasion rather than demanding when dealing with the leader, are able to conceptualize the big picture of their part in the leadership process, have foresight to think beyond the moment, understand their role within the organization as a steward, are committed to the growth of the leader and other followers around them, and build community within the organization by following biblical principles of giving, loving, and serving one-another. This servant spirit is even more manifest when those served respond in similar fashion to the one serving. Leadership scholar, Bruce Winston, accentuates this point by expanding Patterson's servant leadership model to include a reciprocal response from the follower to the leader. Of this response Winston stated:

> The second half of the story occurs when the leader's service results in a change in the follower's sense of love. The follower's Agapao love results in an increase in both the commitment to the leader and the follower's own self-efficacy. The higher levels of commitment and self-efficacy result in a higher level of intrinsic motivation that lead to a higher level of altruism toward the leader and the leader's desire to see the organization do well. This leads to higher levels of service to the leader.[26]

This "second half of the story" of the follower's response closes the loop on the servant leader/follower relationship. Winston's expanded model takes into account the influential role of the follower responding to the servant leader. Winston understands this interaction as a cause-effect relationship between the servant leader upon the follower. The Follower First philosophy would suggest that rather than a linear cause-effect relationship, follower responses are the result of inherent biblical follower characteristics responding to the needs of the Following-Leader who is manifesting servant leader characteristics.

Leading Where You Don't Want To Go

Following-Leaders are known not so much for their gifts, talents, or abilities, as for their hearts that beat with the same desire for the glory of God as that of the Lord Jesus. This is never truer than when the providence of God allows the Following-Leader to enter the crucible of trial. The Bible is replete with references to the difficult plight of the early Christian church and the numerous trials the people went through for the sake of Christ. James wrote that various trials test our faith and produced patience (James 1:2-4). Peter wrote that trials were a testing fire of the genuineness of faith (1 Peter 1:6-9). Paul wrote that through a great trial of affliction the Corinthian church gave liberally (2 Corinthians 8:2). The writer of Hebrews recalls:

> Others were tortured, not accepting deliverance, that they might obtain a better resurrection. Still others had trial of mockings and scourgings, yes, and of chains and imprisonment. They were stoned, they were sawn in two, were tempted, were slain with the sword. They wandered about in sheepskins and goatskins, being destitute, afflicted, tormented — of whom the world was not worthy. They wandered in deserts and mountains, in dens and caves of the earth (Hebrews 11:35-38).

Persevering through trial is the hallmark of the faithful believer. Following-Leaders accept the path set before them by the Lord and seek to glorify God with their responses, all the while seeking to influence others to do the same. This is never more true that when the Following-Leader fills the role of pastor in a local congregation. It is not uncommon for some within the congregation to become disenchanted with the pastor. This process may begin with a perceived snub or a lack of ministry to a family member or dissatisfaction with the Sunday morning messages. More egregious is the person who, because of fear that they will lose power in the church, begins to sabotage the work of the pastor. Regardless of the origins, these detractors begin a process of whittling away the pastor's reputation. This ungodly act of character assassination serves to undermine the pastor's credibility, and if the lies and slander are believed by enough people, the pastor may be asked to resign or fired.

Within these tempest-filled environments, the pastor, as a Following-Leader, has an opportunity to witness to the sovereign supply of the Father. When those employing these despicable tactics expect a similar ungodly response, the pastor can glorify God by not responding in kind, but by blessing those who stand against him. Rather than defend himself, the Following-Leader is willing to place himself in the hands of the Father and remain faithful to the task at hand. The Following-Leader understands that ministry is difficult and there are no guarantees that faithful service will be rewarded with human gratitude.

Additionally, fellow Following-Leaders serving with the pastor (staff members and members of the church), have the opportunity and responsibility to put down rumors and backbiting. As the Apostle Paul wrote in Ephesians 4:29-32:

> Let no corrupt communication proceed out of your mouth, but that which is good to the use of edifying, that it may minister grace unto the hearers. And grieve not the Holy Spirit of God, whereby ye are sealed unto the day of redemption. Let all bitterness, and wrath, and anger, and clamor, and evil speaking, be put away from you, with all malice: and be ye kind one to another, tenderhearted, forgiving one another, even as God for Christ's sake hath forgiven you.

In this passage, as well as others (2 Corinthians 12:20; Colossians 3:8; Titus 3:2; James 4:11; 1 Peter 2:1), it is clear that those who follow the Lord Jesus and the teachings of Scripture will need to be Following-Leaders when it comes to putting down wrath and anger within the Body of Christ. Following-Leaders (I am not talking about pastoral staff here), humbly willing to risk rejection by fellow members will need to confront others of their error for the sake of the unity of the church. In the Follower First philosophy, church discipline is a function and responsibility of the *whole* body. The pastor is not perceived as the spiritual principal to whom every infraction of biblical deportment is brought, but each Following-Leader has the responsibility to immediately address the infraction and gently lead the person in error to confront their sin, repent, and be restored. There may be occasion when the infraction is so egregious within the church body that the Pastor needs to be informed and he and the others leaders need to act. However, Following-Leaders are responsible for addressing common mistakes before they have time to grow into larger problems. Let me quickly add that this responsibility does not create a type of spiritual police state in which some take it upon themselves to police everyone and become someone else's Holy Spirit. On the contrary, within the organization with a Follower First philosophy, all responsibilities are carried out with a spirit of humility, love, and gentleness. The power of submission is exercised and the church operates with an atmosphere of love for the Lord, love for others, and submission to the authority of God's Word. More will be said about this in Chapter 8.

I sometimes tell my ministerial students that I have an idea as to why they are in class being tormented by me and why they are currently serving in difficult situations. The reason is, like me, they prayed a prayer once that went something like this, "Father, I want to be more like Jesus." Now, here we are, serving in difficult situations, being talked about poorly, having people lie about us, gnash their teeth at us, sabotage our plans, and call us just about everything we can imagine. Does that sound a little like how Jesus was treated? Rejoice; we haven't been whipped, beaten over the head with rods, had a crown of thorns placed on our heads or been crucified...at least not yet.

Still, as Following-Leaders, we have been called to serve the Lord Jesus regardless of the circumstances. Jesus said,

> "Truly, truly, I say to you, unless a grain of wheat falls into the earth and dies, it remains by itself alone; but if it dies, it bears much fruit. He who loves his life loses it; and he who hates this life in this world shall keep it to life eternal. If anyone serves Me, let him follow Me; and where I am, there shall My servant also be; if anyone serves Me, the Father will honor him" (John 12:24-26).

If we are to serve Jesus, we are to follow Him. Where He is, there will I, His servant, be. Following-Leaders are servants of the suffering servant. It is little wonder that we should be mistreated because the spirit of those who refused to follow Jesus still remains in some within the church. We have given our lives in service to the Lord. It is His prerogative where He should lead. My role, my honor, is to follow. He may lead me in paths where I would prefer not to travel. Still, the life of the Following-Leader is not directed by preference but by obedience. If it be the will of God, the Following-Leader will serve the Lord in obscurity. He will eschew the cries of friends and family that he is much more worthy of a larger pulpit or a larger responsibility within the church. He will cast aside his own desires that might cry out for recognition from peers, colleagues, or the media. The Following-Leader understands that he is guaranteed one honor, and his recognition will come from only one source, and it is enough to make life worth living. Jesus said, "If anyone serves Me, the Father will honor him." The Following-Leader assumes the same role as that of Paul (Romans 1:1; Galatians 1:10; Titus 1:1), James (James 1:1), and Peter (2 Peter 1:1) who took the appellation "bondservant."[27] These Following-Leaders understood their role was to do the will of their Master, the Lord Jesus Christ. As bondservants they surely followed the same guidelines as those actual bondservants whom Paul instructed to:

... obey in all things your masters according to the flesh, not with eye-service, as men-pleasers, but in sincerity of heart, fearing God. And whatever you do, do it heartily, as to the Lord and not to men, knowing that from the Lord you will receive the reward of the inheritance; for you serve the Lord Christ.

As followers of the Lord Jesus Christ, these bondservants have a reward. Their reward, as for all who follow the Lord Jesus, is the, "Well done" (Matthew 25:21) they will hear from the lips of God the Father.

Conclusion

The Follower First philosophy understands every position within the church as being of extreme importance in the fulfillment of the will of God. Following-Leaders understand their influence is not based upon perceived authority or position within the organization but upon their personal obedience to follow Christ and the Word of God in every endeavor. Gone are the self-assessed excuses for not participating in the life of the church because, "I'm just a layman," or, "I'm just a volunteer." With a Follower First philosophy permeating the church, gone are the self-defeating self-perceptions of inadequacy. It may be true that a particular follower does not have as much talent, personality, or capacity when compared to another. Gratefully, the Follower First philosophy renders this comparison moot because Following-Leaders follow with the talents God has given, influence through the personality God has given, and operate within the church with the capacity God has given. There is no longer any need to look for potential. As one coach for whom I played said, "Potential sits on the bench. I need someone who can play now." Following-Leaders are those who embrace Christ's commands *now*. There is growth to be had emotionally, intellectually, and spiritually. Yet, Following-Leaders act, respond, and obey in the now. They do not wait for when they think they are ready. When God provides the opportunity, they respond. The call is to follow. The response is immediate.

As recognized leaders in the church, Following-Leaders understand that their influence may be manifested through various leadership styles. It will take study and time to sharpen their capacity for influencing others. Still, these leaders recognize the fulfillment of the church's mission is primarily contingent upon those Following-Leaders who serve with the recognized leader. Developing leader styles is important but secondary to followers developing the character, integrity, and consistency of being a biblical follower. It is when these spirit-filled, God-fearing, Christ-loving, followers act in obedience to the word of God they actually live out what it means to be Following-Leaders.

<u>Following-Leaders: The Exercise of Influence</u>

Following Defined

Leading Defined

Increasing Influence
- Love the Perfect Follower
- Apply God's Word
- Love and Seek to Understand People
- Develop Integrity
- Develop Avenues of Influence
  - Charismatic Leadership
  - Transformational Leadership
  - Servant Leadership

Leading Where You Don't Want to Go

Part IV

Develop a Follower Culture

Chapter 7

Embedding a
Follower First Culture

As any young pastor would be, I was thrilled to pastor my first church. I had gone through the candidate process along with my new wife, and the search committee and the church asked me to be the pastor of a new start-up church. I was told by several that the choice was made not so much because of me, but because of my talented and beautiful wife. I have no doubt this is the case.

I was fresh out of seminary and ready to bring the world to Christ. The church was a new mission start and had already suffered some setbacks. The church and I began our journey together amicably enough. The people were supportive and tolerated my new ideas with grace. Of course, being a Baptist church, every decision had to go through a committee of some kind and this slowed decision making to a crawl. Still, we plodded along and the church grew. Finally the day came when I suggested something far outside the congregation's comfort zone.

Growing churches need space, and usually space is a premium. The room in which we conducted our worship services was the largest space in our building, and because we had pews, we could not have any other function in that space. My suggestion was to sell the pews and buy padded, interlocking chairs we could stack during the week and hold mid-week children's events in the same space. Then the fun began. I held meeting after meeting with the church body (about 80 people at the time) explaining the benefits of ministering to others by using the space for more than Sunday worship. Although those in opposition were not vicious, they did have very strongly held opinions and reservations. What will this do to the sanctuary? What about a center aisle for weddings? Won't this have more wear and tear on the carpet? Who will be responsible for moving the chairs? We have never worshipped in chairs before.

Working through the questions, the decision was finally made to sell the pews and purchase chairs. For my remaining four years at the church the chairs functioned exactly as predicted. They were comfortable, functional, and as the church grew, we simply bought more chairs. After five years of ministry, I was offered the opportunity to pastor another start-up church, and I agreed. We left our first church on good terms. Yes, we had had our struggles and our misunderstandings. Some had left the church for various reasons and that hurt me, but my overall assessment of our years of service was positive.

After a few years of ministry in the new church, I had the occasion of being in the city in which my first church was located. I decided to drive by and see what changes had taken place while I was gone. When I arrived, I noticed that things looked the same. The building was locked so I had to look through a window to see inside. When I did, I was shocked to see that in the space where we met for worship the chairs were gone and the pews were back. You can imagine my chagrin when I realized that the change that I led the congregation to adopt was not change at all. It was simply tolerance.

I realize now that the real message behind the questions and the resistance was, "Pastor, we can't really have a church unless we have pews." What I failed to recognize was that although the change for me was functional, the change for the people was cultural. These dear people had a deep seated belief of what worship was and what was required to have worship. They tolerated my wild ideas until I left and then moved back into their cultural norm where things looked like church.

If I could teach one lesson to young seminary students regarding how to operate within the church, I would teach them how to recognize, operate within, and change organizational culture. If I had known that all organizations have a culture, I could have saved myself and those to whom I ministered a tremendous amount of grief and heartache. Every church, whether old or newly planted, has an organizational culture that must be recognized if long-lasting change occurs. In my first church I had successfully changed the furniture, but I had failed to change the culture. If we are to embrace the Follower First philosophy of leading within a church, the change must begin at the deepest level of the church's culture.

What is Organizational Culture?

Initially, I hesitated to introduce this subject. Organizational culture and how to change it are such important aspects to every organization I did not think that a cursory introduction of the subject would do it justice. Yet, if we embrace a Follower First philosophy of ministry in our churches, such a way of looking at life and ministry is so different from the norm that there is no way the church culture would not be impacted. Therefore, the following is a brief overview of how to embed a Follower First philosophy in the church with the hope that you will study the matter in more detail later.

Edgar Schein's work, *Organizational Culture and Leadership*,[1] is the source from which I draw many of these steps to create a Follower First culture. Although Schein posits his insights from a leader's perspective, the Follower First perspective recognizes that every follower in the organization has the responsibility to understand, operate within and, if necessary, change his/her organizational culture. It may be that the recognized leaders of an organization have an advantage in effecting the organization's culture but, as we will see, followers have an important part to play in this process as well.

> Organizational culture is defined as:
> A pattern of shared basic assumptions that was learned by a group as it solved its problems of external adaptation and internal integration that has worked well enough to be considered valid and therefore to be taught to new members as the correct way to perceive, think, and feel in relation to those problems.[2]

Breaking this definition into a few key phrases, perhaps we can gain a better grasp of the idea of organizational culture. The first phrase is, "A pattern of shared basic assumptions that was learned by a group...." When Schein writes of "basic assumptions," he refers to three specific levels of organizational culture.

1. *Artifacts* – "... the phenomena that one sees, hears, and feels when one encounters a new group with an unfamiliar culture."[3] These phenomena include architecture, language, technology and artistic creations. In the church setting we might include pews, stained glass, crosses, certain furniture, etc. as evidence of certain beliefs and assumptions that a group of people have. One must be careful, however, not to draw too many conclusions based on these evidences without investigating the deeper values and assumptions attached to these artifacts.

2. *Espoused Beliefs and Values* – originate through a process where persons agree with a recognized leader what ought to be done, act on that approach and, finding that the approach is successful, incorporate the approach or belief as a part of the organizations 'way of doing things'. The longer these actions continue to work "they gradually become transformed into nondiscussible [sic] assumptions supported by articulated sets of beliefs, norms, and operational rules of behavior."[4] In others words, the espoused beliefs and values

of an organization are the 'That's just the way we do things around here' types of activities and actions that all organizations have. Such espoused beliefs may or may not be congruent with the next level of organizational culture.

3. *Basic Underlying Assumptions* – "the implicit assumptions that actually guide behavior, that tell group members how to perceive, think about, and feel about things."[5] Another way of addressing this level of culture is to recognize this as the organization's predominate world view. Depending on the church, this worldview may be formed by the Bible, the church's history, or even denominational tradition.

It is important to note that this pattern of basic underlying assumptions, according to the definition above, was learned by a group. Each one of us has a personal set of values by which we live our lives and interpret life events. However, it is when individuals of like values gather together as a group for a stated purpose that the group will decide which of the individual group member's values will be incorporated into the DNA of the newly formed organization. Leaders arise from the group because the group is willing to vest certain persons with the responsibility of guarding these congruent values. It is these values that the group adopts as those that can address the next part of the definition.

The group adopts this pattern of shared values because this pattern seems to have "solved its [the organization's] problems of external adaptation and internal integration." When the group initially agrees on shared values for the organization, the organization immediately faces problems related to its existence. The underlying question is, "How will we survive?" This is a question that is faced by every church, whether new or old, and is answered by the group's shared values and assumptions. The question of survival concerns itself with external adaptation; that is, how will the organization relate to and thrive within the surrounding environment. The question of survival also includes issues of internal integration, or, stated another way, how we get along with one another. The issue of survival gives organizational culture its power. This pattern of shared survival values has worked well enough to be considered valid and therefore is taught to new members as the correct way to perceive, think, and feel in relation to those problems. Those who enhance the survival of the organization are lauded and, conversely, those who dare introduce new and untested ideas that might question or contradict previous held values are vilified or rejected because they are perceived as threats against the survival of the organization. Thus, the young pastor who tries to make some changes and cannot seem to make any headway needs to understand that the resistance to change, in some way, is a response to the congregation's desire to survive.

Understand that when change is presented to the church and there is pushback from the congregation, this resistance is more than likely a reflection of the organizational culture. The church culture is a stabilizing factor in the lives of the members and any suggested change results in high levels of anxiety. My suggestion is if you truly want to change a church at its core, it will take time, persistence, and a willingness to endure the misunderstandings of others. Make no mistake; because a Follower First philosophy is antithetical to much of how businesses and churches operate in the United States, if not around the world, you can expect some people initially to embrace the Follower First philosophy, but most will have questions.

For our purpose, organizational culture gives the Follower First individual a necessary perspective regarding how difficult changing a church culture can be. For hundreds of years, churches have been established based upon leader-centered philosophies of operation. It would be unwise to think that such an engrained culture can be changed over night through preaching a few messages on Follower First thinking or teaching Follower First principles of behavior, but this is a start.

One other important aspect of understanding organizational culture allows us to see that resistance to change may be more a product of the prevailing organizational culture rather than, as I unfortunately and naively had assumed, a lack of faith, an unwillingness to respond biblically, or even the devil. I do not mean to imply that the source of resistance may not indeed be from these motivations. What I mean to say is that understanding organizational culture will give those who wish to influence the church an understanding of some people's responses that does not imply some sinister spiritual design. Therefore, we can embrace those who disagree and resist and be patient with them because we know they may simply be battling and fearing for their own and their group's survival.

How Do I Embed a New Culture?

Two key words for embedding a culture are *wisdom* and *understanding*. You might recall that Solomon was asked what he wanted above all things. His response in 1 Kings 3:9-13 was:

> Therefore give to Your servant an understanding heart to judge Your people, that I may discern between good and evil. For who is able to judge this great people of Yours?" The speech pleased the LORD, that Solomon had asked this thing. Then God said to him: "Because you have asked this thing, and have not asked long life for yourself, nor have asked riches for yourself, nor have asked the life of your enemies, but have asked for yourself understanding to discern justice, behold, I have done according to your words; see, I have given you a **wise and understanding** [emphasis mine] heart, so that there has not been anyone like you before you, nor shall any like you arise after you.

Solomon asked for understanding in order to discern between good and evil. God answered his prayer and gave him both wisdom and understanding. Wisdom is "the knowledge and ability to make right choices."[6] Understanding carries the idea of being able "to separate mentally."[7] Applied to our context, if we are to understand our churches, it is imperative that, after thinking critically and separating out what might be espoused values from actual underlying assumptions, we make the right choices. Solomon's grasp of the necessity of wisdom and understanding in dealing with people can be seen in the multitude of times he references wisdom and understanding in the Proverbs.[8] I encourage you to ask God for wisdom and understanding before attempting to influence others at the level of organizational culture. It is not by accident that James, writing with an understanding of the trials of being a follower of Christ, penned these words in James 1:2-8:

My brethren, count it all joy when you fall into various trials, knowing that the testing of your faith produces patience. But let patience have its perfect work, that you may be perfect and complete, lacking nothing. If any of you lacks wisdom, let him ask of God, who gives to all liberally and without reproach, and it will be given to him. But let him ask in faith, with no doubting, for he who doubts is like a wave of the sea driven and tossed by the wind. For let not that man suppose that he will receive anything from the Lord; he is a double-minded man, unstable in all his ways.

Understand Yourself

In order to create real, lasting change, what is needed is to know and better understand the organization beneath the surface. Such understanding comes only as we are willing to invest the time to investigate the core values of the organization and confront the espoused values and underlying assumptions of the church that may be in conflict with Scripture.

How can we discover these core values? Where do we begin? Let me suggest we begin with ourselves. As a Following-Leader, it does me little good to try and discern the values of others when I have not taken the time to address my own values and determine whether or not they are congruent with Scripture. This process of self-introspection can be accomplished if we are willing to be deadly honest with ourselves. Here are a few steps we can take to facilitate this personal values assessment:

1. Set a date on the calendar for a weekend retreat with only you. If we do not set this date and guard it, the other more urgent affairs of our lives will scream too loudly, and we will never find the time to evaluate.
2. Find a quiet place with no phones or televisions. This process will be difficult enough without the constant ringing of phones or temptation to relax in front of the TV.
3. Bring your Bible and a writing pad or laptop to record your thoughts. You will not be able to remember all that comes to mind. Write it down. BE HONEST. Find a biblical validation for each value without taking Scripture out of context. Write down

an application of each value to your life. Write down the consequences that will likely result as you live out your values.

4. Once you have completed your assessment, share your findings with a trusted friend and get his or her input with regard to its accuracy and biblical authenticity.

5. Listen to your friend and ask questions with regard to how your values can be applied in your life.

6. Finally, take the steps necessary to apply your core values in each area of your life.

Done correctly, you are likely to find this values discovery exercise one of the most difficult disciplines you have ever attempted. However, once you have experienced the discord, uneasiness, and quite possibly the pain of discovering and applying your biblical core values to your personal life, you will have some idea of the discord, uneasiness, and pain those in the church will undergo when you ask them to go through this process. Values discovery is not for the faint-hearted. It is a process that needs to be empowered by the Holy Spirit and conducted solely for the glory of God.

Understand the Church

I do not want you to do what I did: waste precious time changing the furniture but not the church. When inheriting an older, established congregation, I often counsel young ministers to be patient and take the time needed to know the people before introducing change. Love them. Seek understanding of the *whys* behind the actions. I realize that a pulpit committee may have told you that the church was ready to grow and make changes, but please realize that a pulpit committee often does not represent the overall underlying assumptions of the congregation. The wise pastor, whether old or young, will take the time to ask good questions of everyone. I might go so far as to say that it might be wise to ask questions of those who might have left the church during the time it was without a pastor. What dynamics took place that precipitated their leaving? Understanding the current organizational culture represents an initial step that must take place before trying to embed a new culture.

For those starting a new church, the same counsel applies. Although the new church will not have a history to investigate, the people who are joining the new work certainly will have a history. It is imperative that you recognize that new ministries are often very attractive to those in other churches who are displaced, discouraged, or even disturbed. Understanding the personal and church histories of those who would join you in the new church is vitally important lest the church with the new culture you wish to plant become subsumed by those who bring their U-Haul trailers of artifacts, espoused values, and basic underlying assumptions to the new work.

Below are a few questions you might want to ask when you are new to an established church or interviewing potential church members when planting a new church:

- **Established:** What is the history of this church?
  New Work: What is your church background?

- **Established:** What activities are of primary importance to you and this church and why?
  New Work: What church activities are of primary importance to you that you might like to see this church participate in and why?

- **Established:** What was the last big change that took place? How was it conducted? How was it received by the church? What were the results?
  New Work: At your last church what was the last big change that took place? How was it conducted? How was it received by the church? What were the results?

- **Established:** What is your view of worship? The Bible? The purpose of the church?
  New Work: What is your view of worship? The Bible? The purpose of the church?

- **Established:** Who are some of the people in the church you respect and why?
  New Work: In your previous church, who are some of the people in the church you respected and why?

- **Established:** How do things get done in this church? Why are they done this way?
  New Work: How should things get done in a church? Why do you believe this is the best way?

- **Established:** What are your personal core values?
  New Work: What are your personal core values?

Understand the Process

The word I would use to describe embedding a Follower First philosophy in the church is *incremental*. Embedding a new way of thinking about how you see the functioning of any organization, much less the church, is a daunting task. In its day, I suppose it may be akin to asking people to consider that the earth is round when the predominate culture was certain the earth was flat, or that the sun is the center of the universe when the prevailing thought was that the earth was the center of the universe. Such scientific assertions are accepted as fact today, but when first introduced they caused massive upheaval. I don't believe the Follower First philosophy to be on the same plain with Copernicus' theories of the universe, nor do I suspect those who hold to a Follower First philosophy will come to the same end as he (burned at the stake). Yet, I don't believe we can be naïve and think that those within the church who exercise control and power based upon a leader-centered philosophy are likely to yield lightly, regardless of the amount of biblical evidence to support the Follower First position. Incremental is the way to proceed.

The beauty of this process is that the change to a Follower First philosophy can begin with any follower willing to exhibit the behaviors of a follower of Christ. What this means is that change within the church can occur through the rank and file membership and does not have to wait upon the recognized leaders to begin making changes. The Follower First philosophy may be more easily disseminated, perhaps, if the leaders in the church were to embrace it. However, as a change agent within the body, I submit that the smallest and the least within the Body of Christ can begin to operate with a Follower First philosophy, and these actions will begin to influence others, who, in turn, will embrace the Follower First way of thinking, perceiving, and acting within the church. In this instance the cliché is true, Follower First thinking is more caught than taught.

Building upon Schein's list of primary embedding mechanisms,[9] I want to broaden this list to include the role followers play in the embedding process. The following steps are the beginning point from which followers can embed a Follower First culture within the church.

Step One:
Pay attention to, measure, and take account of biblical responses.

Developing a system of incentives for people to work toward is a practice that many businesses incorporate to try and motivate their workforce toward greater productivity. In turn, some churches have embraced similar types of systems such as contests to see which Bible study group can raise the most money, have the most new members, or have the highest percentage of attendance. Such contests within the church are intended to be good clean fun and yield results. However, these results are usually short lived as the contest ends and people return to their normal activities which are indicative of their underlying assumptions.

When it comes to motivating people within the church, I suggest we think through the dynamics of what we are actually accomplishing. First, contests do not teach cooperation within the church. They teach competition. You have one group competing against another, and you set up a win-lose scenario. One group will win and get the steak dinner. The other groups will lose and have to serve the group that won. Don't get me wrong. I am not anti-competition. In fact, I am as competitive as they come. However, I believe we have to be careful where we establish competitive cultures, and the church is not one of those areas.

From a biblical perspective, what is the benefit of creating competition within the church? The Bible speaks of loving one another (John 13:34) and encouraging one another to love and good deeds (Hebrews 10:24), but no where have I found that establishing competition within the church is an example of the way Christians ought to work together or become motivated for ministry. One scenario that might work, if you insist on having competitions, is for the group that wins to have the joy of serving the losing groups. This would reflect and embed a more biblical approach where, "If anyone desires to be first, he shall be last of all and servant of all" (Mark 9:35).

A Follower First philosophy seeks to pay attention to and measure faithfulness, not necessarily results. Perhaps we would do well to take account of those who faithfully share their faith, those who encourage others, the person who refuses to spread gossip and slander, or especially those who faithfully teach the truth day in and day out. Such a focus would place the emphasis on the only incentive that truly has lasting results, an unwavering love for the Lord Jesus Christ. Devotion cannot be manufactured. When we see it, we need to recognize these people and pray that their tribe increase.

Step Two:
React biblically to critical incidents and organizational crises.

The one reaction that is primary in a Follower First philosophy is love. Paul said in 1 Corinthians 13, "Love never fails." Love recognizes that all persons within the church are humans and prone to failure. At the same time, the love with which we are to love one another must not tolerate sin. Because the essence of church culture seeks to ensure the survival of the organization, nothing poses a greater threat to the church than a moral failure on the part of a leader or member of the church. The Bible gives guidelines on how we are to lovingly respond to those who have experienced failure, but it is the responsibility of the Follower First believer to make certain that sinful actions are not glossed over or tolerated. As difficult as it may be, church discipline is required if the church is to remain a church and not a social club. Followers are to hold their leaders and each other accountable to the Word of God as the standard for organizational faith and practice. This may require the follower to personally confront the leader and risk rejection. However, from the Follower First perspective, the reputation of Christ is more important than being accepted, and the time may come when, sadly, the follower has to leave the church if the moral failure is not addressed.

Step Three:
Evidence biblical stewardship over all resources.

Leaders are usually given the responsibility of allocating resources to different ministries within the church. As Following-Leaders, it is important that ministries and programs reflecting the core values and mission of the church are financially supported.

On one occasion as a pastor, I became aware of a financial situation in which we were spending more on maintenance than on outreach. Over time, the finance team and I agreed that, although maintaining a beautiful building and campus was important, it should not exceed the outreach portion of our church budget. Adjustments were made so that outreach and missions ministries would be funded first. As a result, the church made the decision to move from a culture of maintaining and surviving to growing and thriving. A new organizational culture was birthed that moved the focus of the church from self to others and guaranteed that money would always be available to those who wanted to reach others with the gospel.

Followers understand that all resources are from the Lord and are to be used to bring Him glory. What resources they are given are welcomed with gratitude and should be used wisely. This attitude of gratitude rather than grumbling is a powerful influence in the lives of those within their sphere of influence.

Step Four:
Model, teach, and coach from a Follower First perspective.

The best way to influence the culture of an organization is to be a Follower First. When given the opportunity to serve others, serve from a Follower First perspective. When teaching others, emphasize the aspects of what it means to be a follower of Christ first in all things. Let the people see you in the way you respond, speak, listen, and live. When others come to you for assistance and advice, share with them the freedom you have being a Follower First. Being a *real* person before others gives you a credibility by which others may desire to embed these same characteristics in their lives.

Step Five:
Receive rewards and status as temporal and fleeting.

More than likely, as a Follower First you will get noticed by others and be given positions of responsibility within the church. After all, who is not going to notice the humble servant, the tireless worker, and the person with a loving demeanor who supports the direction and purpose of the church? As you gain responsibility however, never forget that you are a Follower First. Our place as followers of Christ will be a constant reminder of the humility we must have if we are to influence others. Additionally, any accolades need to be received with an eternal perspective. Nothing on this earth is eternal except the Word of God and the souls of men. Paul had this eternal perspective when in 2 Timothy 4:8 he wrote:

> For I am already being poured out as a drink offering, and the time of my departure is at hand. I have fought the good fight, I have finished the race, I have kept the faith. Finally, there is laid up for me the crown of righteousness, which the Lord, the righteous Judge, will give to me on that Day, and not to me only but also to all who have loved His appearing.

Step Six:
Support those who evidence a Follower First philosophy.

Unlike the teaching from the leadership literature, we are not looking for particular people with potential. Everyone in the church is a candidate to participate in the Follower First philosophy. By holding each other accountable, each follower can encourage and promote the work of those who embrace the Follower First philosophy.

It is important to reiterate that these six steps outline not only what Follower First followers can do but who Follower First followers are. We are to be the people who serve others, take note of the faithful, evidence stewardship, respond biblically, model, teach, coach, and seek the good of others over ourselves. By being this person, we influence the entire organization toward a Follower First philosophy.

Step Seven:
Give the process time.

Being patient and working with others to make the needed changes may be the most difficult step. Internal organizational changes often move at the speed of glaciers. The weight and importance of organizational culture requires that it change slowly. For those seeking to embed a Follower First philosophy, do not become discouraged. It may be that you are in your church for the specific reason of beginning a process that another will complete.

Conclusion

Whether you are ministering in an existing church or beginning a new one, the process of embedding an organizational culture is the most important determiner of whether or not a church will fulfill its purpose. Every follower needs to recognize and understand the aspects of the church's culture in order to make substantive changes that will last a lifetime. A Follower First organizational culture can only be fully embedded as every person identifies himself or herself as a Follower First rather than the leadership position they may hold.

Internal organizational changes often move at the speed of glaciers. The weight and importance of organizational culture requires that it change slowly. For those seeking to embed a Follower First philosophy, do not become discouraged. It may be you are in your church for the specific reason of beginning a process that another will complete. Continue to be a Follower First, and God will use you as a catalyst for change.

Embedding a Follower First Culture

Organizational Culture

How to Embed a Culture
- Understand Yourself
- Understand the Church
- Understand the Process
  - Pay attention to, measure, and take account of biblical responses.
  - React biblically to critical incidents and organizational crises.
  - Evidence biblical stewardship over all resources.
  - Model, teach, and coach from a Follower First perspective.
  - Receive rewards and status as temporal and fleeting.
  - Support those who evidence a Follower First philosophy.
  - Give the process time.

Chapter 8

Identifying
Follower First Behaviors

In order to establish a greater understanding of the Follower First philosophy of leading, I sought to codify a group of behaviors, supported by Scripture that identify those who operate with a Follower First type of thinking. With this desire in mind, I developed the Follower First Profile (FFP) that identifies two categories of biblical follower behaviors: (a) relationship oriented behaviors and (b) responsibility oriented behaviors. Additionally, the Biblical Follower Profile identifies five specific biblical follower behaviors: (a) commitment to the leader, (b) intimacy with the leader, (c) faithfulness and/or loyalty, (d) obedience and/or supporting, and (e) persistence and/or consistency. By using the FFP, each follower can determine his or her level of biblical following and construct a plan to improve areas of weakness and more readily use areas of strengths.

Relationship Oriented Behaviors

One of the unique qualities of Christianity is that the worship of God involves more than mere servitude. The Bible teaches that God loves the world (John 3:16) and reconciles the world in relationship to Himself through the follower's faith in the life, death, and resurrection of His Son, the Lord Jesus Christ (2 Corinthians 5:18; Romans 5:10). During Jesus' earthly ministry, He emphasized this relational aspect of belief and worship by speaking of those who follow Him as "friends" (John 15:14). This relationship aspect is further emphasized when Jesus, speaking metaphorically of those who believe upon Him, said, "My sheep hear my voice and I know them, and they follow Me" (John 10:27). Jesus even defined eternal life in terms of relationship: "And this is eternal life, that they may know Thee, the only true God and Jesus Christ whom Thou hast sent" (John 17:3).

Relationship oriented behaviors revolve around certain relational factors. The call to, "Follow Me" taken in its historical context is a call to walk in close physical proximity with the Savior. Today, even though it is impossible for followers to walk in close physical proximity, it is not impossible to walk in close spiritual proximity. Of this closeness Jesus said, "I will never leave you nor forsake you" (Hebrews 13:5). It is through these and other statements of the Lord Jesus we can deduce the Savior's desire for continuing a deepening relationship with His followers. This deepening relationship manifests itself through specific follower behaviors.

Commitment to the Leader

As we have studied, the primary word in the New Testament for *follow* is *akoloutheo* (ακολυθὲω). This compound Greek word is formed from the prefix *a* which expresses union, or likeness, and the root word, *keleuthos*, which means *a way*.[1] Thus, a possible reading of this term could yield the construct of someone going in the same way. The term is used 77 times in the Gospels and always refers to following Christ. The term *follow* is sometimes used in the literal sense of actually following Christ (see Matthew 4:25) as well as metaphorically with the concept of discipleship (see Mark 8:34, 9:38, 10:21).

The New Testament concept of following as "commitment to the leader" is demonstrated by the disciples, Peter and Andrew, when, at the command of Jesus to follow Him, they, "…immediately left their nets and followed [Jesus]" (Matthew 4:20). John the Baptist declared his commitment to the Lord when he said, "He must increase and I must decrease" (John 3:30). Peter's walking on the water (Matthew 14:28) is another example of one who is committed to the leader, even to the point of risking one's own life. These sometimes radical and counter-intuitive actions on the part of the follower indicate a level of commitment to the leader regardless of personal cost.

Intimacy with the Leader

In the New Testament, the disciples of Jesus were identified as those who were closely associated with Jesus. On one occasion, Peter and John, had been accused by the religious leaders and together, had given a strong defense of their activities. The Scriptures note that, "when [the religious leaders] saw the courage of Peter and John and realized that they were unschooled, ordinary men, they were astonished and they took note that these men *had been with Jesus*" [emphasis mine] (Acts 4:13-14). Jesus emphasized this close proximity of relationship with His followers when before ascending into heaven he told His disciples, "I am with you always, even to the end of the age" (Matthew 28:20). The follower's understanding of intimacy with Christ appears to engender a sense of oneness that Christ seeks to have with His followers. Thus, Christ can say to his followers, "I will not leave you as orphans; I will come to you. After a little while the world will behold Me no more; but you will behold Me; because I live, you shall live also. In that day you shall know that I am in My Father, and you in Me, and I in you" (John 14:18-21). This willingness to be taught by Christ and to apply His words to one's life is indicative of those who continue to grow in an intimate relationship with the Savior.

Responsibility Oriented Behaviors

Relationship oriented behaviors are complimented by responsibility oriented behaviors. From a biblical perspective, the idea of relationship naturally results in the follower having certain responsibilities toward the leader. This concept was emphasized when Jesus stated, "He who has my commandments and keeps them, he it is who loves me, and he who loves Me will be loved by My Father, and I will love him, and will disclose Myself to him" (John 14:21). Additionally, Jesus made the connection between relationship and responsibility when He said, "You are My friends if you do what I command you" (John 15:14). The following responsibility oriented behaviors evidence a life that is truly committed to following the Lord Jesus.

Obedience

The Greek word, *epakoloutheo*, is a compound Greek word. The root word for follow (*akoloutheo*) is preceded with the prefix *epi*, a preposition with the meaning *upon*. This prefix allows the word to be translated with the idea of following after or close upon a person or a concept.[2] The Apostle Peter expresses this concept in 1 Peter 2:21 when he wrote, "For you have been called for this purpose, since Christ also suffered for you, leaving you an example for you to follow in His steps...." This concept of following after Christ is further clarified by Peter's continuing statements in chapter 2 verse 22 describing the person and activities of Christ:

> Who committed no sin, nor was any deceit found in His mouth; and while being reviled, He did not revile in return; while suffering, He uttered no threats, but kept entrusting Himself to Him who judges righteously; and He Himself bore our sins in His body on the cross, that we might die to sin and live to righteousness for by his wounds you were healed.

From the context of these verses it is clear that Peter was aware that followers who are obedient to the commands of Christ would experience suffering and hardship. Obedience to the commands of Christ in the face of hardship, suffering, and even persecution are based upon the follower's understanding of the sovereignty of God and that God the Father would always judge righteously.

A similar Greek word, *parakoloutheo*, is also a compound Greek word that uses the root word for follow *(akoloutheo)* with the prefix *para* which signifies "to follow close up, or side by side, hence, to accompany or to conform."[3] The word is used to describe character qualities that accompany believers who are sharing the gospel and following good doctrine in their lives and ministries. This idea is conveyed in 2 Timothy 3:10 when the apostle Paul proclaims, "You followed my teaching, conduct, purpose, faith, patience, love, perseverance...." It is clear that obedience to the commands of Christ and the teaching of the Scriptures is indicative of a follower of Christ.

Faithfulness
The New Testament often speaks of the abiding faithfulness of God (1 Corinthians 1:9; 2 Corinthians 1:18; 1 Thessalonians 5:24; 2 Thessalonians 3:3) and has many references to faithfulness being a characteristic of those who follow Christ (see Ephesians 1:1; 6:21; Colossians 1:2; 4:9). Paul stated in 1 Corinthians 1:2, "It is required in stewards that a man be found faithful." The Greek word *pistos* is often translated *faithful* but may also carry the meaning of trustworthiness.[4] Followers are entrusted with the gospel of Jesus Christ, gifts of the Spirit, positions of responsibility within the church, and the name of Jesus. A person's faithful stewardship of these constructs is an indicator of their faithfulness to the Lord. Those in the Bible who have been designated faithful are those whose lives have given evidence of keeping a promise and being diligent in their service to others in the name of Christ (Timothy - 1 Corinthians 4:17; Tychicus – Ephesians 6:21; Epaphras – Colossians 1:7; Onesimus – Colossians 4:9; faithful men – 2 Timothy 2:2). Faithfulness is an indispensible characteristic of a follower of Christ.

189

Persistence

Exakoloutheo, is another compound Greek word that takes the root word for follow *(akoloutheo)* and precedes it with the Greek prefix, *ek*, which is the Greek word for *out*. This creates a word that carries the idea of following certain teachings *out* to their end. Peter presents this concept in the negative by stating that the apostles did not "follow cleverly devised tales when we made known to you the power and coming of our Lord Jesus Christ..." (2 Peter 1:16). From this negative statement, we can imply the positive that Peter and the other apostles *did* follow out to the end the accurate teachings of the Lord Jesus.

The Greek word *dioko* has two meanings. The first denotes *driving away* in the sense of persecution. The second means "to pursue without hostility, to follow after."[5] In this second sense, the word describes the means by which followers of Christ are to pursue the character of Christ. To that end, followers are directed to follow: (a) that which is good (1 Thessalonians 5:15), (b) righteousness (1 Timothy 6:11), (c) peace with all men and holiness (Hebrews 12:14), and (d) righteousness, faith, love, and peace (2 Timothy 2:22). The intensity of the verb is captured when *dioko* is translated, "I *press on* toward the goal for the prize of the upward call of God in Christ Jesus" (Philippians 3:14). Persistence is a behavior of all who follow. However, let me be quick to add that persistence includes recognizing our complacency and mediocrity in the things of God. Once recognized, the persistent follower is quick to confess these to the Lord and continue to pursue the Lord Jesus Christ.

What Would Other People Think?

Because the FFP is a self-report instrument, there is the possibility that "respondents may answer questions in such a way as to represent themselves favorably...[thus] the validity of self-reports becomes suspect as the amount of self-presentation increases relative to self-disclosure."[6] To evaluate the respondent's tendency to give socially desirable responses, the FFP incorporated five questions which have been validated as a social desirability response set. These questions are added to the FFP to assess our capacity to assess ourselves. As followers of Christ, we need to be honest with God, ourselves, and those whom we serve, in that order. These questions help measure how much we may be looking over our shoulder and wondering what other people think.

I measured the face validity[7] of the Follower First Profile and have used it with many different churches in many different contexts. I present a portion of the survey in Figure 9 and invite you to complete one free copy of the entire thirty-five item profile with answer sheets by accessing www.followerfirst.com and entering the code listed on page 233 of this book. Additional copies of the profile may be purchased for use in your church or Christian based organization through Heartworks Publications, www.heartworkspublications.com.

The Follower First Profile

The primary measurement of the Follower First Profile (FFP) is a person's commitment to following Christ. In the Follower First philosophy this commitment to Christ is a prerequisite for following other leaders in the church.

The response options in the FFP are worded so that positive responses produce higher numerical values using a five-item response ordinal Likert scale. The terms used for the responses are, to little or no extent, to a slight extent, to a moderate extent, to a great extent, and to a very great extent. These responses relate to a numerical scale of 1 to 5 respectively. A lower score would indicate a lower presence of biblical follower behavior and a higher score would indicate a higher presence of biblical follower behavior.

The answer sheet allows the person completing the FFP to identify strengths and weaknesses in their own follower quotient and develop a personal plan for enhancing the indicated strengths and strengthening the indicated weaknesses.

Figure 9: Follower First Profile
Instructions
Each of the following survey statements describes a particular behavior of a follower of Christ. Read each statement carefully and circle the response that best describes to what extent that statement accurately characterizes your actual behavior. Each response relates to a numerical scale of 1 to 5: (1) to little or no extent, (2) to a slight extent, (3) to a moderate extent, (4) to a great extent, and (5) to a very great extent.

	to little or no extent	to a slight extent	to a moderate extent	to a great extent	to a very great extent
1: In my work I serve Christ.	1	2	3	4	5
2: I pray to God through Christ throughout the day.	1	2	3	4	5
3: I confess my sins to Christ.	1	2	3	4	5
4: I obey Christ regardless of the circumstances.	1	2	3	4	5
5: I am consistent in telling others of Christ.	1	2	3	4	5
6: I am consistent with my spiritual disciplines of prayer, Bible reading and Scripture memory.	1	2	3	4	5
7: I obey Christ because of my love for Him over all things.	1	2	3	4	5
8: I always obey Christ.	1	2	3	4	5
9: I have a daily quiet time of fellowship with Christ.	1	2	3	4	5
10: I serve Christ where I live.	1	2	3	4	5

Applying the Follower First Profile to the Church

The Follower First Profile measures follower behaviors as they relate to following after Jesus Christ. One might ask, "How can these behaviors be applied when, as a part of the Body of Christ, we are called upon to follow leaders within the church?" My initial response is... very carefully. Although there are many wonderful church leaders in the world, there are still charlatans and fakes who capture people with slick presentations, supposed special knowledge, and/or promises of blessing and success. Paul warns of these people even in the first century church:

> But know this, that in the last days perilous times will come: For men will be lovers of themselves, lovers of money, boasters, proud, blasphemers, disobedient to parents, unthankful, unholy, unloving, unforgiving, slanderers, without self-control, brutal, despisers of good, traitors, headstrong, haughty, lovers of pleasure rather than lovers of God, having a form of godliness but denying its power. And from such people turn away! For of this sort are those who creep into households and make captives of gullible women loaded down with sins, led away by various lusts, always learning and never able to come to the knowledge of the truth. Now as Jannes and Jambres resisted Moses, so do these also resist the truth: men of corrupt minds, disapproved concerning the faith; but they will progress no further, for their folly will be manifest to all, as theirs also was. (2 Timothy 3:1-9)

As a follower of Christ, I am commanded to follow only those persons whom God has called to lead His church, not those who presume to lead His church. As the above scripture stated, the non-leaders or self-called individuals will be revealed over time because they will refuse to follow the Lord Jesus Christ and obey His commands. Therefore, before I follow anyone, I must know as best I can who the leaders follow. This will not be learned simply from what the leaders say, but what they do over time. I don't have to have a personal conversation with the leader to determine whom he/she is following, although a personal conversation is a good place to start. All I need do is observe their lives. Whom human leaders follow is the best indicator of how they will lead and whether they ought to be leading in the first place. As a follower, it is always my choice whether or not I will follow. I call this the follower's prerogative. If over the course of a few months the leader appears intent on following the Lord, I will put in my lot with the leader and follow.

Commitment

Follower First pastors are desperately looking for believers who are committed to the Lord Jesus Christ and His church. The work of ministry is just that: work. The work requires a commitment on the part of the member that goes beyond good intentions. Church members need to be committed to their leaders. However, in this cynical world, this is very difficult. One way for members to be committed to their leaders is by remembering the One to whom we can fully commit ourselves, the Lord Jesus.

When we get involved in our churches, we should join a congregation with the understanding that this is the place where we are entrusting our most important aspect of living, our spiritual livelihood. By understanding what it means to be a biblical follower, perhaps we can begin to change the perspective of many that the church is merely another organization that can help us raise our kids, entertain our students, marry our adult children, and bury us when we die. As a committed follower, I will trust Jesus to have oversight of His church, His bride. I will never be a part of a church that is not led by persons who are not sinners forgiven by the grace of God. This fact will always be in the back of my mind. However, I will also keep in the forefront of my thinking that the church, its people and its leaders, are all followers operating ultimately under the sovereign hand of an almighty God. I can always trust God. I can expect to be disappointed by my human leaders many times. However, my primary commitment is to Christ, and He never disappoints.

Intimacy

Intimacy is another word we do not use very much with regard to our church leaders. Our busy worlds make it difficult to find the time to slow down and spend time with our leaders. The same is true for the leader. How can one person take a meal with hundreds, if not thousands, of people? Such an expectation is not feasible, and if a follower has this expectation, he or she is going to be disappointed and may be guilty of placing an expectation on the leader that the Bible does not. Church leaders are commanded to care for the flock. How they do this is not spelled out in the Scriptures, and if we place an expectation from our own personal lives or from a traditional cultural perspective on what it means for the pastor to care for us, then we will be operating outside the Bible and will find ourselves not following Christ in the process.

There are ways the follower can be intimate with the leader. Emails that simply say you are praying for the leader, short notes through the mail, making certain that the church appreciates her ministers regularly are just a few ways we can bless our leaders and build intimacy with them. It is appalling the number of churches that never recognize the loving care given by their ministers. We muzzle the ox (1 Timothy 5:18) when it comes to gaining intimacy with our leaders. Many pastors and church leaders tell me that the greatest intimacy is built when church members participate in ministry activities. Witnessing, visitation, mission trips are all available for the follower if he or she wants to rub shoulders with their leaders.

The most important activity of intimacy with the leader is praying for the leader. Asking for prayer from the leader, praying for the leader on the spot, and praying for the leader in your personal prayer time, all lead to a greater intimacy. As followers of Christ we want our leaders to hunger after intimacy with Christ. Giving our leaders time to have that intimacy is a blessing to the leader. However, there is little time for extended personal devotion if the pastor is expected at the hospital, nursing home, funeral home, baseball game, visitation, business committee, etc. If prayer is our vital life, as followers of Christ we need to be certain of our prayers, and we need to make certain our leaders have time to pray. We do not want to be guilty of expecting our leaders to minister to us before our leaders have time to minister before God in prayer. We love our leaders when we don't require our leaders to beckon to our every call. Let us seek to take our leaders to the prayer closet with us in praying for them before we require them to meet with us.

Obedience

Obedience: The word sounds rather harsh doesn't it? Yet, in God's economy, obedience is the currency of love. Jesus said that if we love Him we will obey His commandments (John 14:21). If I love Christ I will obey His commands. If I love my leaders I will obey them. When the writer of Hebrews 13:17 said "Obey those who rule over you, and be submissive, for they watch out for your souls, as those who must give account. Let them do so with joy and not with grief, for that would be unprofitable for you," the Holy Spirit used a Greek word translated obey that carries the meaning of having confidence in those who lead.[8] Followers are to assent to the positional authority of those who have the responsibility before God of watching over their souls. By having confidence in God, the follower of Christ can have confidence in the God called leader as long as the leader has given proof of being a follower of Christ and His Word. Follower obedience to the leader results from: (a) the leader's integrity in following the Lord and (b) follower trust in the sovereignty of God.

I can recall one of several instances during my years as a pastor that the church had come to a place of decision. In one instance, the church had out grown the old church building we had rented, and I desired the church to move from a typical church type building in order to conduct services in the local high school auditorium. After several weeks, it may have been months of discussion, the church decided to follow my lead, leave the confines of the smaller church building, and move our weekend services to the high school cafeteria. The result was that the people grew closer together because the decision required us to move sound equipment and all our materials from storage to the school each Sunday morning. You do gain intimacy with people while you are serving the Lord. Also, the extra space allowed us to have more visitors. The parking was almost unlimited, and we saw the church continue to grow.

I share this story because after several years, one of the older members of the congregation and I were talking and he related a story of how he came to grips with the whole idea of moving the church to the school. This gentleman confided that he was not too keen on the idea from the start. He participated in the discussions. He read the material presented, but this was not convincing. What convinced him was the consistency he saw in me and the desire God had placed in my heart to reach the people of our community, even to the point of making ourselves uncomfortable. His words to me were, "I didn't have any confidence in you because you were just a young whipper-snapper. But I did have confidence in God and what He wanted to do in our community and because of that, I agreed to go." That is being a biblical follower. The church made a decision to follow me only because they had the confidence in God that reaching people even at the expense of their own comforts was what God had called them to do. It appeared on the surface that they were obeying me and my wishes when in reality, they were obeying God. I can't tell you how glad I am that I was actually following the Lord's lead with that idea.

Faithfulness

The concept of faithfulness carries with it the idea of keeping a promise. As followers of Christ, we have been entrusted with the treasure of the gospel of Jesus Christ (2 Corinthians 4:7). As good stewards we faithfully share this gospel with others (1 Corinthians 4:1-2). Even though this is our duty as servants of Jesus Christ, we gladly carry out this duty and others from a heart of love for the Savior.

With this backdrop of loving responsibility, followers of Christ have the joy of being faithful to others within the church. From my own experience as a pastor, I can say that nothing is more gratifying than to have a member of the church commit to perform a certain work and then have them complete the task without being reminded, begged, or cajoled into compliance. The faithfulness of the follower to complete a task is one way we can bring joy to the hearts of those who lead.

As Followers First, we must understand that our commitment to a task within the church is more than just a task we hope to fulfill for the leader. We are actually making a commitment to the Lord to perform a work for His church. Followers are people who follow through on their commitments. When followers make a promise, followers keep a promise.

Persistence

One key to determining perseverance and persistence is to ask the question, "What will it take to make me quit?" Follower First believers understand that all churches are composed of humans and that there is no perfect church. Followers understand that leaders in the church will make mistakes and they will sometimes disappoint. However, as long as the mistakes are not of a moral nature nor violate clear biblical teaching, staying in a fellowship of believers for the long haul is a gift that the leaders greatly appreciate. Standing beside the leader through difficult times and not cutting and running at the first sign of trouble usually results in a bond of friendship with the leader that leads to even greater degrees of intimacy and trust.

I recall fondly those friends who were members of my churches who decided to stand with me during difficult times. When seeking to grow a new church, it is all the more important to find those persons who will persist through the difficult, embryonic times that new churches go through as they mature. I still treasure their persistence that evidenced their faithfulness to Christ, His church, and me. It was a persistence that was based on a love for the Savior and a desire to see the church succeed. As we have already stated, followers hold the keys to whether the leader succeeds or not. By both leader and followers being present through the good and bad times, the likelihood of growing a healthy church increases.

Conclusion

How can a person really tell if someone has a Follower First philosophy? I hope the Follower First Profile will be a starting point for discovery. However, the truth is that we can never truly know the thinking, the philosophy, or the worldview of a person until we have spent time with them through good times and bad. In fact, it is through the bad times that we are more likely to see the true thinking of another. It is one thing to be a Follower First kind of person when it is popular, everyone likes you, the church is going well, and people are happy. But what happens to our thinking when we see people taking advantage of our generosity or not giving us the benefit of the doubt? What happens when the people with whom we work and minister do not hold to the same biblical ethic we do and begin to act in ways that dishonor God? What happens when being a follower costs us something dear, like a relationship, or our reputation, or even our job? Then we will know if we are truly Followers First.

Identifying Follower First Behaviors

Relationship Oriented Behaviors
- Commitment to the Leader
- Intimacy with the Leader

Responsibility Oriented Behaviors
- Obedience
- Faithfulness
- Persistence

The Follower First Profile

Chapter 9

Following
Can Change the World

It was a very good question. The student asked if there were any biblical examples of a church operating according to Follower First principles. The question gave me pause to think of another question. Are there any biblical examples of a church operating according to the leadership principles often applied today? In other words, does anything in the New Testament give us reason to think that the pastor/teacher and/or elders who ministered in the New Testament churches were vested with the responsibility of getting a vision from God for the ministry, developing a mission statement, and relating this vision to the rest of the church body for it to accomplish? Were they commissioned to set the pace for the ministry, oversee programs, make certain staff members do their jobs, plan new buildings, form the budget and administrate the office? Historically, the Bible gives evidence that when God wanted to do a work, He chose an individual to begin the process. Moses, Nehemiah, and Paul are all examples of this. Yet, God's working through Old Testament patriarchs and New Testament apostles does not necessarily support the idea that instilling vision and mission in one person is God's model for the New Testament church. In the absence of any direct teaching regarding leaders' *organizational* responsibilities in the church, it appears the members of the church have added this template to a list of responsibilities for ministers to accomplish that simply does not have the weight of Scripture behind it. In fact, I would argue that there is more evidence for a Follower First philosophy of operation within the New Testament church than what is currently exercised today.

Acts chapter six indicates one instance in which an organizational problem was remedied by choosing certain men to serve those who were being neglected. From an organizational perspective, it appears the apostles knew their main concern was the ministry of the Word of God. Therefore, they instructed the believers to choose seven men to serve and remedy the problem.

Consider Paul's letters to the churches. A broad view of these letters reveals that most of them were corrective in nature. Having been established by Paul in his missionary journeys, these churches were now being led by elders whom the apostle established to oversee the spiritual well-being of those who were coming to faith in Christ. Most of what Paul shares with Timothy and Titus are directives on how to establish spiritually minded leaders, not organizational duties. I have found nothing that suggests that the elders were charged with the sole responsibility of discerning the will of God for the church, but that their primary responsibility was to make certain that the Gospel and the doctrines were taught and practiced without compromise or adulteration.

Given that these elders/pastors obviously would be looked upon to help in making decisions for the church, how would such decisions be made? Those who operate with an elder rule system may say that the elders are charged with decision making and that they will discern the will of the Lord for the church and inform the church with regard to ministry direction. Those who operate with a congregational rule system may say that each member of the congregation would come to a decision and then the majority would rule. I contend that neither of these systems completely conveys the desire of the Lord for His church.

In a leader-centered organizational culture, an elder rule system has the potential of discounting the input and influence of members of the church who might be able to add insight into the decision making process. Similarly, a congregational rule system has the potential of discounting the input of pastors and deacons and relying solely upon parliamentary procedure and majority rule to discern the will of God. The Follower First philosophy, on the other hand, moderates the possible authoritarianism of an elder rule system and the possible political positioning of a congregational rule system, bringing the church organizational decision making into line with the Lord's establishing the church as a body of followers participating with followers in the process.

We have already seen how a Follower First philosophy begins with the premise that all born again members of the Body of Christ are followers of Christ first. By remembering this simple but fundamental truth, the church can engage more persons in ministry activities and make a greater impact on the culture and community. By leveling the playing field of ministry, the invisible wall of separation between clergy and laity is lowered so that all can understand and fulfill their responsibilities as followers of Christ.

Within a Follower First church, decisions can be made more quickly and with less friction. This is due largely to the congruence already present within the group with regard to core values, mission, and vision. By emphasizing following and followers, the church body can rally around her common purpose as given by the Lord Jesus Christ to make disciples of all nations. Within the Great Commission, the church has her mission statement, "Make disciples." The authority of the Lord Jesus Christ and the Bible give the core values of how church business and ministry are conducted. The vision is the world-wide influence of "all nations." The only need for the church is clarifying the strategic details of how to fulfill the vision. When the church is unified with regard to mission, core values, and vision, she becomes a powerful force of change within the local community and around the world.[1] Lives are changed and the church grows numerically and spiritually as a natural result of the unity of the Body.

Sometimes there may be occasion when the Body cannot come to a unified decision on how to fulfill a specific ministry endeavor. Well meaning followers on each side of the decision may simply have a difference of opinion on what needs to be done and how. When time in prayer and corporate conversation yields nothing by way of agreement, what is to be done?

In these times, I would suggest exercising the power of submission. Rather than cause a schism in the church, followers could choose to defer to those who are in positions of oversight (i.e. elders, pastors). The Follower First philosophy does not support a consensus type of leadership. Those in positions of leading others sometimes have to make the difficult decisions. The Follower First philosophy does not abrogate this responsibility but seeks to involve as many people in the decision making process as possible. When the time comes to make a decision, those who lead will be responsible to make it. Entrusting the decision to these fellow followers in leader positions and then praying for them can bring about unity within the Body. In addition, once the decision is made, actively supporting the decision, even though it may not have been one's idea, will bless the Body of Christ and honor the Lord. Unanimity may not be possible, especially for large churches. However, unity can be accomplished when followers choose to follow the Lord and trust their fellow followers with the decision.

Followers Making History

It amazes me to this day how the church has survived through the centuries. The pages of church history are a testimony to the faithfulness of God to sustain His Son's Bride. We know the names of the more famous who, in some extraordinary way, were used of God to preach revival, establish churches, or simply stand for truth. However, let us not forget that for every famous follower, there are tens of thousands of unnamed souls who have changed the world simply by being who God had called them out of the world to be: followers of Christ.

Followers change history. They may be called leaders by writers, but in reality, they are followers. With the courage of their convictions they are willing to stand against all odds in order to maintain their personal integrity and the reputation of Christ. The eleventh chapter of Hebrews highlights the saints of old. Their place in the Hall of Faith is not granted because of their station as leaders, but because of their faithful following.

Abraham faithfully followed the command of God to sacrifice Isaac, believing that God would raise him from the dead (Hebrews 11:19). Moses' parents faithfully followed the law of God and not the law of Pharaoh and thus, Moses was spared. Moses followed the directives of the Lord and kept the Passover, sparing the lives of the people of God. This list goes on and on. Yet, all of these faithful followers died without seeing the promise of the Messiah fulfilled. By the grace of God, we have seen the fulfillment.

Today, these great saints become for us a great cloud of witness cheering us on as we run the race set before us with endurance.

> Therefore we also, since we are surrounded by so great a cloud of witnesses, let us lay aside every weight, and the sin which so easily ensnares us, and let us run with endurance the race that is set before us, looking unto Jesus, the author and finisher of our faith, who for the joy that was set before Him endured the cross, despising the shame, and has sat down at the right hand of the throne of God (Hebrews 12:1-2).

Our primary objective is to look to Jesus and follow Him. We lead the next generation only as they follow our lead. Whether they follow or not will be their choice, their prerogative. Our choice is now. Will we follow the Lord and revel in our following? Will we assuage any thought of position or power and find ourselves fulfilled in humbly following the commands of Christ? Like the saints of old, this journey will require an undying faith. The future of the church depends on those who follow the perfect follower, the Lord Jesus Christ.

How Do You Measure Up?

From what we have studied, it is evident that the Bible views the church as a follower-centered organization. Biblical followers have responsibilities that must be fulfilled if the church is to accomplish her mission. The Follower First philosophy offers a way for believers to view themselves within the church that gives meaning and purpose to each individual member.

Below are a Follower Covenant and a Following-Leader Covenant. There are 65 organizational responsibilities followers have within the church. The Following-Leader Covenant contains 26 additional organizational responsibilities for those who hold the position of leader in the church. The number of responsibilities indicates the important role followers within the church.

Follower Covenant

As a follower of Christ I will:

- Be totally committed to the Lord Jesus Christ.
- Answer Christ's imperative and not simply volunteer.
- Assume responsibility.
- Talk to my leaders and not about them.
- Initiate action.
- Serve and serve alongside my leaders.
- Be a trustworthy member of the team.
- Serve Christ by serving others.
- Unburden my leaders where I can.
- Stand up for my leaders.
- As much as possible, seek to make ministry a joy for my leaders.
- Not have unreasonable expectations of my leaders.
- Challenge my leaders to greatness.
- Risk my personal relationship with my leader to protect the character and reputation of Christ.
- Embrace change and encourage others to do the same.
- Give insight to the change process.
- Focus on the future rather than dwell in the past.

- Change internally, spiritually, and emotionally.
- Have an expectant attitude toward the future.
- Lovingly correct my leaders if they violate or stray from the Word of God.
- Not lead a rebellion against my leaders.
- Not play the martyr.
- Leave the church and find another in which to serve if the immoral/unbiblical actions of the leaders go unchecked.
- Act on biblical grounds instead of cultural or personal preferences.
- Be totally dependent on Christ and seek to grow in the image of Christ.
- Do my work heartily as unto the Lord, rather than men.
- Finish the work I am assigned.
- Use my gifts to fulfill the mission of the church to the glory of God.
- Study, learn, and apply the teachings of the Word of God.
- Not succumb to the temptation of self-preservation.
- Not allow anger to dictate my actions.
- Get the facts from the source before forming opinions or conclusions.
- Seek reconciliation with my leaders and fellow followers.
- Seek the unity of the Spirit in the bond of peace.
- Not seek peace at any price but be a peace keeper.
- Be actively engaged with my leaders and the church.
- Be good stewards of all that God has given.
- Become a critical thinker regarding what I read and hear.
- Hold no expectation of leading, regardless of what position I might hold in the business world.
- Trust the promises of God's Word.
- Do the work of an ambassador.
- Fulfill my ministry of reconciliation by sharing the Gospel.
- Die to self and live to Christ.
- Be diligent to use my power to the glory of God.
- Give my resources to assist my leader to accomplish the organizational goals.

- Not succumb to operating with a quid-pro-quo.
- Establish an organization culture of grace.
- Overcome the status quo.
- Not simply comply with my leader's requests.
- Trust God by being committed to my leaders.
- Be a follower with integrity.
- Not repay evil for evil.
- Live peaceably with all men.
- Not avenge myself.
- Overcome evil with good.
- Place Christ's reputation above my own.
- Follow in the power of the Holy Spirit.
- Exercise the power of submission.
- Seek my "well done" from God, not men.
- Discipline my life toward intimacy with the Lord Jesus Christ.
- Put other followers before me.
- Persist in following Christ.
- Follow-through on my commitments.
- Keep my promises.
- Be a Following-Leader.

Following-Leader Covenant

As a Following-Leader I will:

- Assume all the responsibilities and characteristics of a follower of Christ.
- Follow the leading of the Lord Jesus Christ and the Word of God.
- Submit to the authority of Jesus and the Word of God.
- Accurately interpret the teaching of the Word of God.
- Create environments in which followers are encouraged to share their insights.

- Create an environment of trust where the fear of reprisal does not exist.
- Respect all followers of Christ.
- Teach and oversee the biblical responsibilities of followers.
- Encourage followers to lead in appropriate contexts.
- Not fear the involvement of followers in the decision making process.
- Not seek to hold on to my position.
- Cherish the interdependent relationship with followers.
- Lead through the power of submission.
- Accurately assess my own frailties and infirmities.
- Lead with humility.
- Serve Christ by serving my followers.
- Be the first to die to self and live for Christ.
- Be diligent to use my power to the glory of God.
- Not operate with a quid-pro-quo.
- Establish an organizational culture of grace.
- Trust God by trusting and being committed to my followers.
- Be a leader of integrity.
- Place Christ's reputation above my own.
- Lead in the power of the Holy Spirit.
- Make prayer a primary function of my position.
- Keep my promises.

I will answer the command of my Leader to

FOLLOW ME!

ENDNOTES

CHAPTER ONE

[1] NT:2758 keno/w **kenoo** (ken-o'-o); from <u>NT:2756</u>; to make empty, i.e.
(figuratively) to abase, neutralize, falsify:
KJV - make (of none effect, of no reputation, void), be in vain.
Biblesoft's New Exhaustive Strong's Numbers and Concordance with
Expanded Greek-Hebrew Dictionary. Copyright © 1994, 2003
Biblesoft, Inc. and International Bible Translators, Inc.

[2] NT:190 akoloutheo (ak-ol-oo-theh'-o); from NT:1 (as a particle of union) and
keleuthos (a road); properly, to be in the same way with, i.e. to
accompany (specially, as a disciple): KJV - follow, reach. Biblesoft's
New Exhaustive Strong's Numbers and Concordance with Expanded
Greek-Hebrew Dictionary. Copyright © 1994, 2003 Biblesoft, Inc. and
International Bible Translators, Inc.

[3] NT:1205 deute (dyoo'-teh); from NT:1204 and an imperative form of eimi (to
go); come hither!: NT:3694 opiso (op-is'-o); from the same as
NT:3693 with enclitic of direction; to the back, i.e. aback (as adverb or
preposition of time or place; or as noun): KJV - after, back (-ward),
(+get) behind, follow. Biblesoft's New Exhaustive Strong's Numbers
and Concordance with Expanded Greek-Hebrew Dictionary. Copyright
© 1994, 2003 Biblesoft, Inc. and International Bible Translators, Inc.

[4] Instances of the use of the word "come" (duete pisow)
Matt 11:28-30
Come to Me, all *you* who labor and are heavy laden, and I will give you
rest. Take My yoke upon you and learn from Me, for I am gentle and
lowly in heart, and you will find rest for your souls. For My yoke *is*
easy and My burden is light."
Matt 22:4-5
Again, he sent out other servants, saying, 'Tell those who are invited,
"See, I have prepared my dinner; my oxen and fatted cattle *are* killed,
and all things *are* ready. Come to the wedding."'
Matt 25:33-34
And He will set the sheep on His right hand, but the goats on the left.
Then the King will say to those on His right hand, 'Come, you blessed
of My Father, inherit the kingdom prepared for you from the
foundation of the world:

Matt 28:5-6

But the angel answered and said to the women, "Do not be afraid, for I know that you seek Jesus who was crucified. He is not here; for He is risen, as He said. Come, see the place where the Lord lay.

John 4:29

"Come, see a Man who told me all things that I ever did. Could this be the Christ?"

John 21:12-13

Jesus said to them, "Come *and* eat breakfast." Yet none of the disciples dared ask Him, "Who are You?" — knowing that it was the Lord.

Rev 19:11-18

Now I saw heaven opened, and behold, a white horse. And He who sat on him *was* called Faithful and True, and in righteousness He judges and makes war. His eyes *were* like a flame of fire, and on His head *were* many crowns. He had a name written that no one knew except Himself. He *was* clothed with a robe dipped in blood, and His name is called The Word of God. And the armies in heaven, clothed in fine linen, white and clean, followed Him on white horses. Now out of His mouth goes a sharp sword, that with it He should strike the nations. And He Himself will rule them with a rod of iron. He Himself treads the winepress of the fierceness and wrath of Almighty God. And He has on *His* robe and on His thigh a name written:

KING OF KINGS AND LORD OF LORDS.

Then I saw an angel standing in the sun; and he cried with a loud voice, saying to all the birds that fly in the midst of heaven, "Come and gather together for the supper of the great God...

CHAPTER TWO

[1] Barna Research Grouphttp://theologica.blogspot.com/2005/06/how-many-americans-really-attend.html and http://www.barna.org/FlexPage.aspx?Page=Topic&TopicID=10

[2] Kelley, Mark (2008) http://www.bpnews.net/bpnews.asp?Id=28197

[3] http://media.umcom.org/umcorg/2007/State_of_the_Church/Final_SOTC%20BOOKLET.pdf, p. 9

[4] We are inadvertently short-circuiting the ministry of the Church by our use of terms that do not accurately portray the activity we are called to act upon. We create ships and isms that are made up of different activities and we call those these discipleship, evangelism, leadership. Because

we have created them as intellectual, academic types of constructs, they have lost their biblical thrust. Inspection of the scriptures shows that the bible knows nothing of discipleship or evangelism. These are constructs which have been extrapolated from the Word. The Bible teaches much about following, disciple making, leading, and evangelizing. However, when we seek to capture the essence of these activities by making them a list of prescribed activities, the life inherent in the active participle form and verbal noun (gerund) aspect of the word is killed. The construct becomes sterile. We begin to look upon the activities as the fulfillment of the command rather than the actual product of the activity. Discipleship becomes a prescribed number of meetings and plans and memorized outlines instead of the actual product of an obedient disciple. One might argue that these activities are a means to and end. However, most churches who say they are concerned with discipleship would point to the number of discipleship classes rather than point to the number of disciples. The same might be said for evangelism. This is not to say that classes and activities surrounding the process of disciple making are wrong. It is to say that classes for such purposes simply to give us cause to pat ourselves on the back and say that we are fulfilling the Great Commission is an exercise in self-aggrandizement. I propose we do away with such false constructs and stay with the biblical terms of making disciples, evangelizing and leading. Then, when we are asked to give an account, we will not point to our activities but rather to the activity that the Lord has already prescribed.

Leadership does not exist in the Scriptures. Leading does exist. The idea is that there is a complete, definable list or group of concepts and activities that indicate these areas is a construction that is pressed upon the Scriptures. What we are left with are anecdotal assertions of one person's way of acting within a particular context. There are no didactic teachings on leading and how to lead. Writers and pastors must extrapolate principles that appear to make sense and then apply them to a current context. When this is done often enough, we have a tendency to codify many of these principles and ascribe to them merit. We are prone to want to declare THIS is leadership. Such declaration s may give us comfort and closure on the idea of what leaders are supposed to do. However, to codify one list is to leave out the dimensions of another's list. Then we have dueling lists of concepts and ideas regarding what leadership is. Leadership scholars have written a paper outlining over 200 definitions and ideas on what leadership is. Others state that many of the leadership theories we are discussing today are still the same concepts that have been discussed through the last half century. The reasons for all these discussions may be due to the fact that leading can be identified but leadership varies with regard to context. Do servant leaders have an advantage over transformational leaders? Or is serving others merely an expression of how to be a transformational leader? The concepts of leading and following may be too fluid to be captured within the pages of a book. The best I can ask of you is that you consider looking at life from a different perspective. Embrace who you are as a follower FIRST. Don't succumb to the fear of not becoming the leader that everyone seems to teach is the penultimate goal of life. Be the person God has created you to be and then act according to His best interest in the positions of responsibility He gives.

[5] McIntosh, Gary L. (2003). Biblical Church Growth. Grand Rapids: Baker Books, p. 39. Knowledge gained through general revelation is God's truth. It is true because it is sourced in the life-giving God. As such, it is biblical to make full use of empirical research in the fields of anthropology, sociology, and other sciences. Why? Because God's general revelation reflects his character; it is intelligible, coherent, and discoverable. Truth discovered from the natural realm of creation, human development, and history is God's truth held in common with all people – believing and nonbelieving. We are free to explore, discover, and use common truths.

[6] Maxwell, John C. (1995). Developing the Leaders Around You. Atlanta: Thomas Nelson Publishers, p. 7.

[7] Ibid. p. 10

[8] Maxwell, John C. (1993). *Developing the Leader Within You.* Atlanta: Thomas Nelson Publishers, p. 58

[9] Maxwell, John C. (1998). *The 21 Irrefutable Laws of Leadership.* Nashville: Thomas Nelson Publishers. p. 36.

[10] Ibid. p. 51.

[11] Ibid. p. 136.

CHAPTER THREE

[1] Chaleff, Ira. (1995). *The Courageous Follower.* San Francisco, CA: Barret-Koehler Publishers, Inc.

[2] Bible Knowledge Commentary/Old Testament Copyright © 1983, 2000 Cook Communications Ministries; Bible Knowledge Commentary/New Testament Copyright © 1983, 2000 Cook Communications Ministries. All rights reserved.

[3] Kelley, Robert (1992) *The Power of Followership*, New York, Doubleday Currency.

[4] Kelley, Robert (1988). In Praise of Followers. *Harvard Business Review*, p. 146.

[5] Ibid. p. 143

[6] Rost, Joseph (1991) *Leadership for the Twenty-first Century*. Praeger, New York, New York.

[7] Ibid. p. 108

[8] Ibid. p. 109

[9] Rost, p. 109

[10] Ibid. p. 109

[11] Ibid. p. 10

[12] Hughes, R. L., Ginnett, R. C., & Curphy, G. J. (2006). *Leadership: Enhancing the Lessons of Experience*. Boston: McGraw-Hill/Irwin, p. 12.

[13] http://scidiv.bcc.ctc.edu/MATH/Mobius.html   This curious surface is called a **Möbius Strip** or Möbius Band, named after August Ferdinand Möbius, a nineteenth century German mathematician and astronomer, who was a pioneer in the field of topology. Möbius, along with his better known contemporaries, Riemann, Lobachevsky and Bolyai, created a non-Euclidean revolution in geometry. Möbius strips have found a number of surprising applications that exploit a remarkable property they possess: one-sidedness. Joining A to C and B to D (no half twist) would produce a simple belt-shaped loop with two sides and two edges -- impossible to travel from one side to the other without crossing an edge. But, as a result of the half twist, **the Möbius Strip has only one side and one edge!** To demonstrate this, (1) start midway between the "edges" of a Möbius Strip and draw a line down its center; continue the line until you return to your starting point. Did you ever cross an edge? (2) Next, hold the edge of a Möbius Strip against the tip of a felt-tipped highlighter pen. Color the edge of the Möbius Strip by holding the highlighter still and just rotating the Mobius Strip around. Were you able to color the entire edge?

CHAPTER FOUR

[1] WORSHIP. The act of paying honor to a deity; religious reverence and homage. The rendering of the following Heb. and Gk. words:
1. Heb. shaha (to "bow down"), to prostrate oneself before another in order to do him honor and reverence (Gen 22:5; etc.). from The New Unger's Bible Dictionary. Originally published by Moody Press of Chicago, Illinois. Copyright (c) 1988.

[2] Used with permission, Faith, Prayer, & Tract League: Tract #76; Grand Rapids, MI 49504

CHAPTER FIVE

[1] One source to consider is the article on AUTHORITY IN RELIGION International Standard Bible Encyclopedia

[2] Ivancevich and Matteson (2002). *Organizational Behavior and Management.* McGraw-Hill, New York, New York. p. 389

[3] Ibid. p. 389.

[4] The New Unger's Bible Dictionary. Originally published by Moody Press of Chicago, Illinois. Copyright (c) 1988.

[5] NT:1849 exousia (ex-oo-see'-ah); from NT:1832 (in the sense of ability); privilege, i.e. (subjectively) force, capacity, competency, freedom, or (objectively) mastery (concretely, magistrate, superhuman, potentate, token of control), delegated influence. KJV - authority, jurisdiction, liberty, power, right, strength.Biblesoft's New Exhaustive Strong's Numbers and Concordance with Expanded Greek-Hebrew Dictionary. Copyright © 1994, 2003 Biblesoft, Inc. and International Bible Translators, Inc.

[6] Ivancevich and Matteson. p. 388

[7] Montoya, A. D. (1995). In *Rediscovering Pastoral Ministry*, John MacAuthur, p. 287

[8] Means, James E. (1989). Leadership in Christian Ministry. Grand Rapids: Baker, p. 97

[9] Malphurs, A. and Will Mancini (2004). *Building Leaders*. Grand Rapids: Baker Books, p. 86

[10] Clinton, J. Robert (1988). *The Making of a Leader*. Navpress, p. 167

[11] The types of power mentioned in this section are taken from Ivancevich & Matteson, *Organizational Behavior and Management*. McGraw-Hill, New York, New York p. 388-393

[12] NT:2634 katakurieuo (kat-ak-oo-ree-yoo'-o); from NT:2596 and NT:2961; to lord against, i.e. control, subjugate: KJV - exercise dominion over (lordship), be lord over, overcome. Biblesoft's New Exhaustive Strong's Numbers and Concordance with Expanded Greek-Hebrew Dictionary. Copyright © 1994, 2003 Biblesoft, Inc. and International Bible Translators, Inc.

[13] Ivenecivich & Matteson, p. 392

[14] For further study:
Romans 2:2 - Romans 2:8 -, 1 Corinthians 13:6 - 2 Corinthians 4:2 - 2 Corinthians 6:7 - 2 Corinthians 11:10 - 2 Corinthians 12:6 - Galatians 2:5 - Galatians 2:14 - Galatians 3:1 - Galatians 4:16 -Galatians 5:7 - Ephesians 1:13 -Ephesians 4:15-Ephesians 4:21-Ephesians 4:25 - Ephesians 5:9 - Ephesians 6:14 - Philippians 1:18 - Colossians 1:5 - Colossians 1:6 - 1 Thessalonians 2:13 - 2 Thessalonians 2:10 - 2 Thessalonians 2:12 - 2 Thessalonians 2:13 - 1 Timothy 2:4 - 1 Timothy

2:7 - 1 Timothy 3:15 - 1 Timothy 4:3 - 1 Timothy 6:5 - 2 Timothy 2:15 - 2 Timothy 2:18 - 2 Timothy 2:25 - 2 Timothy 3:7 - 2 Timothy 3:8 - 2 Timothy 4:4 - Titus 1:1

[15] http://www.lectlaw.com/def2/q003.htm

[16] Ivenecivich & Matteson, p. 392

[17] http://www.merriam-webster.com/dictionary/statusquo

[18] The idea of compliance may also be a cause for so many disillusioned people who 'walk the aisle' or 'prayed the sinners prayer', thinking that by complying with the request of the preacher, friend, or mother, that this was what it means to be saved. There is no commitment of heart to Christ only compliance with a prescribed set of actions. Responding to Christ's call to salvation is an act of obedience not merely compliance. Perhaps we would do well to make certain that those who are responding to the gospel know the difference.

[19] 1 Corinthians 16:16; Ephesians 5:22; Colossians 3:18; James 4:7; 1 Peter 2:13; 1 Peter 5:5

[20] NT:3401mimeomai (mim-eh'-om-ahee); middle voice from mimos (a "mimic"); to imitate:KJV - follow.(Biblesoft's New Exhaustive Strong's Numbers and Concordance with Expanded Greek-Hebrew Dictionary. Copyright © 1994, 2003 Biblesoft, Inc. and International Bible Translators, Inc.)

IMITATE, IMITATOR
A. Verb. mimeomai NT:3401, "a mimic, an actor" (Eng., "mime," etc.), is always translated "to imitate" in the RV, for KJV, "to follow," (a) of imitating the conduct of missionaries, 2 Thess 3:7,9; the faith of spiritual guides, Heb 13:7; (b) that which is good, 3 John 11. The verb is always used in exhortations, and always in the continuous tense, suggesting a constant habit or practice. Vine's Expository Dictionary of Biblical Words, Copyright (c)1985, Thomas Nelson Publishers)

[21] Consider the following:
1 Corinthians 4:16
Wherefore I beseech you, be ye followers of me.
1 Corinthians 11:1
Be ye followers of me, even as I also am of Christ.
Ephesians 5:1
Be ye therefore followers of God, as dear children;
1 Thessalonians 1:6
And ye became followers of us, and of the Lord, having received the word in much affliction, with joy of the Holy Ghost:
1 Thessalonians 2:14

For ye, brethren, became followers of the churches of God which in Judaea are in Christ Jesus: for ye also have suffered like things of your own countrymen, even as they have of the Jews:

Hebrews 6:12

That ye be not slothful, but followers of them who through faith and patience inherit the promises.

1 Peter 3:13

And who is he that will harm you, if ye be followers of that which is good?

[22] I am grateful to my colleague, Brad Arnett, Ph. D. for his insights regarding this passage of Scripture.

[23] Kouzes, J. M, & Posner, B.Z. (1995). *The Leadership Challenge*. San Francisco: Jossey-Bass, p. 22.

[24] 1 Chron 29:14 For man of himself can give nothing: "What am I, and what is my people, that we should be able to show ourselves so liberal?" kowach (OT:3581) `aatsar (OT:6113), to hold strength together; both to have power to do anything (here and 2 Chron 2:5; 22:9), and also to retain strength (2 Chron 13:20; Dan 10:8,16; 11:6), only found in Daniel and in the Chronicle. hitʰnadeeb (OT:5068), to show oneself willing, especially in giving. kaazo't (OT:2063) refers to the contribution to the building of the temple (vv. 3-8). From Thy hand, i.e., that which is received from Thee, have we given. From Keil & Delitzsch Commentary on the Old Testament: New Updated Edition, Electronic Database. Copyright (c) 1996 by Hendrickson Publishers, Inc.

[25] Sanders, J. Oswald Spiritual Leadership p. 79.

[26] Ibid. pp 81-82.

CHAPTER SIX

[1] Northouse, Peter (2007). *Leadership Theory and Practice*. Thousand Oaks, CA: Sage Publications, Inc.

[2] Maxwell, John C. (1995). D*eveloping the Leaders Around You.* Thomas Nelson Publishers, Atlanta, Georgia, pp. 47-60.

[3] See http://www.ichthus.info/Disciples/intro.html

[4] Murray, Andrew (1981) *With Christ in the School of Prayer*. Springdale, PA: Whitaker House, p. 7.

[5] Maluphurs, Aubrey (2004). *Values-Driven Leadership*. Grand Rapids: Baker Books, p. 44.

[6] Compassion - NT:4697 splagchnizomai (splangkh-nid'-zom-ahee); middle voice from NT:4698; to have the bowels yearn, i.e. (figuratively) feel sympathy, to pity:KJV - have (be moved with) compassion. Biblesoft's New Exhaustive Strong's Numbers and Concordance with Expanded Greek-Hebrew Dictionary. Copyright © 1994, 2003 Biblesoft, Inc. and International Bible Translators, Inc.

[7] Russell, R. F. (2001). The role of values in servant leadership [Electronic version]. *Leadership & Organization Development Journal, 22*(2), 76-84. Retrieved October 28, 2004, from ABI/INFORM Global database.

[8] Graen, G. B., & Cashman, J. (1975). A role-making model of leadership in formal organization: A developmental approach. In J. G. Hunt & L. L. Larson (eds.), *Leadership frontiers* (pp. 143-166). Kent, OK: Kent State University Press.

[9] Northouse, Peter G. (2007). *Leadership Theory and Practice*. Thousand Oaks, CA: SAGE, p. 159.

[10] Weber M. (1947). The theory of social and economic organization (T. Parsons, Trans.) New York: Free Press.

[11] Kouzes & Posner, (1995). *The Leadership Challenge*. San Francisco: Jossey-Bass.

[12] House, R. J. (1976). A 1976 theory of charismatic leadership. In J. G. Hunt & L. L. Larson (Eds.), *Leadership: The cutting edge* (pp. 189-207). Carbondale Southern Illinois University Press.

[13] Taken from Northhouse, P. G. (2007). Leadership Theory and Practice. Thousand Oaks, CA: SAGE, p. 178-179

[14] Burns, J. M. (1978). *Leadership*. New York: Harper & Row.

[15] Northouse, Peter G. (2007). *Leadership Theory and Practice*. Thousand Oaks, CA: SAGE, p. 176.

[16] Bass, B. M. (1985). *Leadership and performance beyond expectations*. New York: Free Press.

[17] Northouse, Peter G. (2007). Leadership Theory and Practice. Thousand Oaks, CA: SAGE, p. 181=182

[18] Ibid p. 183

[19] Ibid p. 183

[20] Ibid p. 183

[21] Greenleaf, R. K. (1977). *Servant leadership: A journey into the nature of legitimate power and greatness*. New York: Paulist.

[22] The Understanding and Practice of Servant-Leadership - Spears
http://www.regent.edu/acad/sls/publications/conference_proceedings/servant_le
adership_roundtable/2005/pdf/spears_practice.pdf

[23] For a complete explanation of these constructs see: Servant Leadership Research Roundtable – August 2003, 7
http://www.regent.edu/acad/sls/publications/conference_proceedings/servant_le
adership_roundtable/2003pdf/patterson_servant_lead ership.pdf

The following excerpts are from this article, used with permission.

Agapao – Love is the cornerstone of the servant leadership/follower relationship, specifically *agapao* love, which according to Winston (2002) is *agapao* love, or the Greek term for moral love, meaning to do the right thing at the right time and for the right reasons. *Agapao* love means to love in a social or moral sense and includes "embracing the judgment and the deliberate assent of the will as a matter of principle, duty, and propriety" (p. 5). This is in deep contrast to the idea that servant leadership is merely a subset of transformational leadership where the focus of the leader is on the organization, or organizational objectives. Servant leadership stands alone in regard to this follower focus. This type of love applies to today's leaders, in that leaders must consider the needs of their followers. This love is shown by leaders who consider each person as a total person -- one with needs, wants, and desires. *Agapao* love is alive and well in organizations today and it is the foundation for what Winston (2002) calls the "platinum rule" (or do unto others as they would want you to do). *Agapao* love is consistent with servant leadership to the extent that servant leaders must have such great love for the followers that they are willing to learn the giftings and talents of each one of the followers. The leader that leads with *agapao* love has a focus on the employee first, then on the talents of the employee, and lastly on how this benefits the organization

Humility - Humility is the ability to keep one's accomplishments and talents in perspective, which includes self-acceptance, and further includes not being self-focused but rather focused on others (Sandage & Wiens, 2001). Humility, therefore, is a peaceful virtue that rejects self-glorification (Lawrence, 2002). Bower (1997) linked servant leadership with the unassuming behavior of being humble; he believed that humility is a necessity for chief executives, or leaders. The virtue of humility causes one to consider moderation, to listen to the advice of others, and to come with the realization that the right use of power means rejecting the dictatorial (Harrison, 2002).

Altruism, according to Monroe (1994), is not merely having good intentions or being well-meaning; altruism is more about concern for the welfare of another. DeYoung (2000) also concurred with the traditional view of altruism as an unselfish concern for others often involving personal sacrifice; however, he believed that the personal pleasure derived from helping others should also be included in our understanding of altruism. In contrast, Hattwick (1986) placed altruism at one end of the spectrum with personal self-interest at the other end. Altruism seeks the fulfillment of others with behavior directed toward the benefit of others and identifies this behavior as consistent with servant leadership.

Bishop Desmond Tutu, Sam Walton, Mother Teresa, and Princess Diana are among Sosik's (2000) examples of altruistic people.

Vision. Vision is most often regarded as the organizational vision, or a vision of the future destination of the organization. However, Patterson (2003) offers the servant leader's focus is on the individual member of the organization and the vision component is about how the organizational members future state. This vision refers to the idea that the leader looks forward and sees the person as a viable and worthy person and seeks to assist each one in reaching that state. Harvey (2001) saw this same ability as inherent in Greenleaf's (1977) formulation of servant leaders as healers, making the person whole by helping that person to because they help others attain the larger vision or purpose than they otherwise might be able to attain for themselves. This visionary process includes seeing each person's unique gifts and influences the decisions of the leader and helps the leader shape a plan for the future, all while asking if the people are being served. Patterson (2003) states that servant leaders learn to know people's abilities and see where they are headed in order to serve them. The visionary servant leader also is able to know the followers and help them develop a clear sense of purpose, direction, dignity and direction (Batten, 1998). Servant leaders enrich lives, build better human beings, and encourage people to become more than they ever believed, and that this is more than a job; this deep-rooted leadership is about mission, the mission to serve (Melrose, 1995).

Trust is a building block for servant leaders (Patterson, 2003), one that is an important element for the servant leader (Wis, 2002); this is due to the belief of the servant leader in trusting in others, which produces a standard of excellence for the entire organization. Respect for and goodwill towards others is the foundation on which trust is built, which is built on goodwill towards others according to Fairholm and Fairholm (2000); further, without trust, discord and disharmony exist. Fletcher (1999) advocated that servant leadership's basis is trust, which is supported by Kezar (2002) who described a servant leadership philosophy as helping people to feel comfortable and creating an open environment where everyone has a voice, and everyone works collaboratively and collectively while using skills such as truth telling. Russell (2001) concurs, noting that trust is essential for servant leaders and that the values of integrity and honesty build interpersonal and organizational trust and leads to credibility. Patterson (2003) offers that trust is a building block to work from for servant leaders, a trust in the unseen potential of the followers, believing they can accomplish goals, a self-fulfilling prophecy. Story (2002) agrees, noting that trust is an essential characteristic of the servant leader.

Empowerment. Greenleaf has been called "the father of the empowerment movement" because empowerment is one of the most important characteristics of servant leadership (Buchen 1998; Russell & Stone 2002). Veronesi (2001) explained that there is no servant leadership where there is no sharing of power. Empowering people, with the best interest of those served in mind, is at the heart of servant leadership (Veronesi; Kezar 2002). Empowerment is entrusting power to others, really giving it away (Patterson, 2003); and involves effective listening, making people feel significant, putting an emphasis on teamwork, and valuing of love and equality (Russell & Stone, 2002). In addition, servant leaders also empower by teaching and developing people (Russell & Stone). The servant leaders' satisfaction comes from the growth of others and that they are willing to hold themselves accountable for the results (Blanchard, 2000). Bennett (2001) stated that servant leaders need to know their followers and understand their needs for the knowledge and experience that they acquire through empowerment. Farling, Stone, and Winston (1999) stated that servant leaders empower followers in accordance with acting on their values and that this relationship is transforming. The idea of empowerment and servant leadership go hand in hand, in that servant leadership puts an emphasis on service, a wholistic approach to work, personal development, and shared decision-making (Lee & Zemke, 1993). Empowering followers is a major goal of servant leaders, who desire to create many leaders at all levels (Russell, 2001). Melrose (1995) believed that servant leadership involves giving people chances to move into new and more powerful roles by preserving their roots, respecting their value, and preserving their dignity. In this empowerment-rich model of servant leadership, the leader empowers followers to find their own paths, and they, in turn, are inspired to help others find their best paths. Empowerment involves helping clarify expectations, goals, and responsibilities, and even more importantly it means letting people do their jobs by enabling them to learn, grow, and progress, and it means allowing for self-direction and freedom to fail; all of this multiplies the followers' strengths and trust (Melrose, 1995). By empowering followers, servant leaders are allowing them freedom to proceed toward their goals, helping them make dreams reality. Empowerment is giving up control and letting the followers take charge as needed. Throughout this process, the servant leader is channeling followers, is balancing the growth of followers, and is aware of what is best for the follower. This empowerment allows the follower to bloom and grow.

Service. The servant leader gives of ones self in service (Swindoll, 1981) which involves personal involvement and authenticity. Service is giving of oneself and requires generosity which can mean giving of time, energy, care, compassion, and perhaps, even one's belongings. Servant leaders exhibit service as they support the frontline, discover the uniqueness of each employee, unleash creativity in people, and contribute to the larger good knowing that this is bigger than themselves, and further, actually seek to opportunities to serve others (Aggarwal and Simkins, 2001; Lyerly & Maxey, 2001; Wis, 2002; Smith, 2003; Patterson, 2003). The servant leader is a role model, in behavior and styles, showing others in the organization how to serve, setting the organizational climate (Lytle, Hom, & Mokwa, 1998; Lynn, Lytle, & Bobek, 2000). Melrose (1995) stated that when this type of example is set, service begets service, ultimately permeating the corporate culture.

[24] Ibid.

[25] Greenleaf, R. K. (1977). *Servant leadership: A journey into the nature of legitimate power and greatness.* New York: Paulist. p. 352.

[26] Winston, Bruce, (2003). Servant Leadership Research Roundtable – August 2003
http://www.regent.edu/acad/sls/publications/conference_proceedings/se rvant_leadership_roundtable/2003pdf/winston_extending_pat terson.pdf

[27] Rom 1:1[A servant] This name was what the Lord Jesus himself directed His disciples to use, as their general appelation; Matt 10:25; 20:27; Mark 10:44. And it was the customary name which they assumed; Gal 1:10; Col 4:12; 2 Peter 1:1; Jude 1; Acts 4:29; Titus 1:1; James 1:1. The proper meaning of this word servant, doulos (NT:1401), is slave, one who is not free. It expresses the condition of one who has a master, or who is at the control of another. It is often, however, applied to courtiers, or the officers that serve under a king: because in an eastern monarchy the relation of an absolute king to his courtiers corresponded nearly to that of a master and a slave. Thus, the word is expressive of dignity and honor; and the servants of a king denote officers of a high rank and station. It is applied to the prophets as those who were honored by God, or especially entrusted by him with office; Deut 34:5; Josh 1:2; Jer 25:4. The name is also given to the Messiah, Isa 42:1, "Behold my servant in whom my soul delighteth," etc.; Isa 53:11, "Shall my righteous servant justify many." The apostle uses it here evidently to denote his acknowledging Jesus Christ as his master; as indicating his dignity, as especially appointed by him to his great work; and as showing that in this Epistle he intended to assume no authority of his own, but simply to declare the will of his master, and theirs. (from Barnes' Notes, Electronic Database. Copyright (c) 1997 by Biblesoft)

CHAPTER SEVEN

[1] Schein, Edgar H. (2004). Organizational Culture and Leadership. Jossey-Bass, San Francisco, CA

[2] Ibid. p. 17

[3] Ibid. p. 25

[4] Ibid. p. 29

[5] Ibid. p. 31

[6] WISE, SKILLED

   Chokmah is the knowledge and the ability to make the right choices at the opportune time. from Vine's Expository Dictionary of Biblical Words, Copyright (c)1985, Thomas Nelson Publishers.

[7] OT:995 biyn (bene); a primitive root; to separate mentally (or distinguish), i.e.(generally) understand: Biblesoft's New Exhaustive Strong's Numbers and Concordance with Expanded Greek-Hebrew Dictionary. Copyright © 1994, 2003 Biblesoft, Inc. and International Bible Translators, Inc.

[8] Consider the following verses in Proverbs regarding understanding:

   Prov 1:2;Prov 1:5;Prov 2:2;Prov 2:3;Prov 2:6;Prov 2:11;Prov 3:5;Prov 3:13;Prov 3:19;Prov 4:1;Prov 4:5; Prov 4:7;Prov 5:1;Prov 6:32;Prov 7:4;Prov 7:7;Prov 8:1;Prov 8:5;Prov 8:14;Prov 9:4;Prov 9:6;Prov 9:10; Prov 9:16;Prov 10:13;Prov 10:13;Prov 10:23;Prov 11:12;Prov 12:11;Prov 13:15;Prov 14:29; Prov14:33; Prov 15:14;Prov 15:21;Prov 15:32;Prov 16:16;Prov 16:22;Prov 17:18;Prov 17:24;Prov 17:27;Prov 18:2;Prov 19:8;Prov 19:25;Prov 20:5;Prov 21:16;Prov 21:30;Prov 23:4;Prov 23:23; Prov 24:3;Prov 24:30; Prov 28:2;Prov 28:11;Prov 28:16;Prov 30:2

[9] Schein, p. 246

- What leaders pay attention to, measure, and control on a regular basis
- How leaders react to critical incidents and organizational crises
- How leaders allocate resources
- Deliberate role modeling, teaching, and coaching
- How leaders allocate rewards and status
- How leaders recruit, select, promote, and excommunicate

CHAPTER EIGHT

[1] International Standard Bible Encyclopedia (1996). Biblesoft Electronic Database.

[2] Ibid

[3] Ibid

[4] Strong's Exhaustive Concordance (1994). Biblesoft Electronic Database.

[5] International Standard Bible Encyclopedia (1996). Biblesoft Electronic Database.

[6] Hays, R. D., Hayashi, T., & Stewart, A. L. (1989). A five-item measure of socially desirable response set. *Educational and Psychological Measurement, 49*, 629-636. Retrieved November 15, 2006, from SAGE Social Science Collections Database, p. 629.

[7] Validity

The Follower First Profile was developed to identify and measure behaviors identified in the biblical literature as belonging to persons who seek to follow after Christ. The BFP employs self-ratings using a forced-choice Likert response. Forced-choice items "do not include responses such as *other, no opinion, not sure, or not applicable* as choices but require respondents to select from among a fixed set of response alternatives" [Dixon, E. N. (2003). An exploration of the relationship of organizational level and measures of follower behaviors. Unpublished dissertation, the University of Alabama in Huntsville, p. 50]. This type of response is popular among researchers [Alreck, P. L., & Settle, R. B. (1985). *The survey research handbook.* Chicago, IL: Irwin.], is easy to count, and allows for multiple sampling of any single factor.

The response options were worded so that positive responses meant a higher numerical value using a five-item response ordinal Likert scale. The terms used for the responses were, to little or no extent, to a slight extent, to a moderate extent, to a great extent, and to a very great extent, which relates to a numerical scale of 1 to 5 respectively. The lower the score would indicate a lower presence of biblical follower behavior and the higher scores would indicate a higher presence of biblical follower behavior. Each of the five characteristics has one reverse coded statement to determine respondent credibility and/or respondent fatigue.

To enhance the content validity of the instrument, a pool of experts was assembled to evaluate the potential assessment items as they related to the operationalized constructs. This pool consisted of a New Testament professor, a homiletics professor, an Old Testament professor, and a leadership professor. Each of these individuals holds a Ph. D. in his field. Each expert was given the literature review and biblical word studies as self-study background material before assessing the accuracy and appropriateness of the assessment items.

Their review of the potential assessment items resulted in several changes. One concern centered on the possibility that the word study of the Greek words could result in a "root fallacy". A root fallacy is described as a "notion that the real meaning of a word is found in its original root" [Duvall, J. S., & Hays, J. D. (2005). *Grasping God's Word*. Grand Rapids, MI: Zondervan, p. 133]. The point was made that the prefixes added to the original root meaning of the word *follow*, did not necessarily result in what would be a literal translation of the Greek word for all instances of the word in the New Testament. Issues of context have a major bearing on the actual translation of the word. It was suggested that the word study be changed to reflect that the Greek words *may* be translated in this manner rather than assert a definitive translation.

Another suggestion resulted in changing statements that reflected more of an attitudinal assessment to statements that assessed specific behavior. Because the FFP is a behavioral assessment tool, it is imperative that all of the statements reflect behaviors. Whereas these behaviors may be based upon certain beliefs and attitudes, there may be occasion when the individual's behaviors are not congruent with the individual's stated beliefs. Therefore, the assessment items were changed to reflect only behaviors.

Additional statements were added so that each construct would be measured by at least six items. There is "widespread acceptance for a ratio of survey item to factors using five or more items per factor to achieve reliable estimates" (Dixon, 2003, p. 54). Additional questions regarding the construct of obedience were added to clarify the motive behind the activity of obedience. Other statements were changed to reflect greater clarity, and the profile items were randomly sorted in order to guard against respondent fatigue. The demographic questions were chosen to allow for cross-sectioning of the survey results from different respondent groups. This will allow for more understanding and value from the survey results [Custom Insight (2006). http://www.custominsight.com/tutorial/survey-using-demographics.asp

To assess the face validity of the instrument, the adjusted FFP was pilot-tested with a group of eighteen Christians composed of ministerial students, pastors, pastor's wives, church members and church staff members. The testing showed that the instrument was simple, straightforward to complete, not time-consuming (approximately six minutes) and generally accepted by the participants. Many of the participants commented on the directness of the statements and how the way the phrasing of the statements did not allow for prevarication. Also, several of the participants commented on how the instrument would be a positive self-assessment tool.

The pilot test revealed that several of the questions needed greater specificity with regard to the subcategory being measured. Suggestions for more specific wording were offered and the changes made to the instrument. Also, the pilot-test suggested an additional demographic question regarding denominational and/or church affiliation would be helpful when making assessments of the findings. The group believed that the answers to some of the questions may be different depending on the theological bias within certain denominations and churches and such a demographic would allow the data to be assessed with regard to these various groups.

The pilot-test revealed that questions regarding the subcategory of *obedience* needed to include additional questions regarding the motive behind a person's obedience. These additional questions were added to clarify the difference between a person's obedience because of intimacy with Christ and a person's duty because of perceived church obligation. The essence of the additional statements is to try and differentiate between obedience with regard to the area of relationship and obedience with regard to legalistic duty. These changes were made to the FFP.

In order to assess the construct validity of the instrument, an exploratory factor analysis would need to be performed to determine if the constructs explained any significant variance in the instrument items. This exploratory analysis "defines the possible relationships in only the most general form and then allows the multivariate technique to estimate relationship(s)... and lets the method and the data define the nature of the relationships [Hair, J. F., Anderson, R. E., Tatham, R. L., & Black, W. C. (1998*). Multivariate data analysis.* Upper Saddle River, NJ: Prentice Hall].

Limitations

The primary limitation of the development of the FFP is that the instrument was developed and pilot-tested by only Baptists and not a variety of Christian denominational representation. This single source for the development of the statements could possibly word items that may be misleading to those in other denominations because of the specificity with which certain words, theological assumptions, and concepts are used within the Baptist faith. To broaden the scope of the applicability of the instrument, Christians from other denominational perspectives should be asked to gauge the content and face validity of the instrument.

[8] NT:3982 pei/qw **peitho** (pi'-tho); a primary verb; to convince (by argument, true or false); by analogy, to pacify or conciliate (by other fair means); reflexively or passively, to assent (to evidence or authority), to rely (by inward certainty): *KJV* - agree, assure, believe, have confidence, be (wax) confident, make friend, obey, persuade, trust, yield. (Biblesoft's New Exhaustive Strong's Numbers and Concordance with Expanded Greek-Hebrew Dictionary. Copyright © 1994, 2003, 2006 Biblesoft, Inc. and International Bible Translators, Inc.)

CHAPTER NINE

[1] Malphurs, A. (2005). *Advanced strategic planning, 2nd edition*. Grand Rapids: Baker.

A
Agapao, 155
Akoloutheo, 22
Angry Followers, 75
Anti-Follower Bias, 47
Assessment, 40, 83, 130, 174
Authority, 103

B
Barna Group, 37
Bass, B. J., 152
Bible, 7, 21, 31, 36, 47
Body of Christ, 9
Bondservants, 104, 162
Burns, J. M., 151

C
Chaleff, Ira, 58, 64
Change, 68, 124, 182
Charismatic Leadership, 150
Christlikeness, 60
Church
  Culture, 49, 123, 169, 172
  Foolish, 12, 128, 145, 147
Commitment, 194
  Faithfulness, 128, 197
  Humility, 129
  Integrity, 127
  Price, 127
  To leader, 186
Compassion, 146
Conflict, 51, 89, 115, 145
Confront, 52, 102, 123, 142,
    161, 179
Consequences, 36
  Church Divisions, 40
  Cavalier Interpretations, 41
  Ineffectiveness, 36
  Member Non-participation, 38

Consensus, 204
Consistency, 164
Cooperation, 102, 178
Courageous Followers, 58, 64
Cross, 12, 83, 93, 128, 130
Culture, 169
  Embed, 167, 169, 173
  Levels, 170
  Quid-pro-quo, 122
  Steps, 178

D
Dependence, 9, 60, 70, 84, 128,
    133, 141
Descriptive, 42
Deute opisow, 28
DNA, 85, 171

E
Elders, 105
Empower, 73, 94
Empowerment, 155, 222
Enable, 133
Equipping, 39
Exemplary Followers, 70
  Commitment, 70
  Competence, 71
  Courage, 71
  Self-Management, 70
Exceptional Disciple, 23
Exousia, 103

F
Faithfulness, 128, 189, 197
Free, 81
Follower First, 8
  Behaviors, 185
    Relational, 186
    Responsibility, 188

K
Kelley, Robert, 69
Knowing God, 142

L
Leader,
  As follower, 50, 108
  Necessary, 49
  Styles, 149
Leader-centered, 36
Leadership, 8, 78
Leading, 7, 8, 17, 51, 78, 100,
131, 138, 142, 159, 204
LMX, 149

M
Maintenance Followers, 77
Malphurs, Aubrey, 107
Matthew, 24
Max Weber, 150
Mediocre Followers, 76
Methodist, 37
Ministry, 88
Mobius Strip, 77
Montoya, Alex, 107
Moses, 46
Murray, Andrew, 144

N
Neutrality, 91

O
Obedience, 27, 43, 61, 126, 141,
  188, 196
Organizational Culture, 8, 10,
  49, 51, 88, 123, 169
  Embedding, 171
  Levels, 170
  Schein, Edgar, 169

P
Paradox, 82
Parents, 105
Pastor, 53
Pastoral Authority, 106
  Accountability, 109
  Consultant, 109
  Responsibilities, 108, 111
  Spiritual, 107
Paternalistic, 64
Patterson, Kathleen, 155
Persistence, 172, 185, 190, 198
Perspective, 47
Peter, 26, 27
Philip, 23
Philosophy, 137
Place, 89
Potential Disciples, 24
Power, 102, 106
  Coercive, 113
  Expert, 115
  Information, 119
  Referent, 116
  Resource, 117
  Reward, 111
  Structural, 116
Power and Control, 49
Power of Submission, 129
Post-Industrial Followers, 72
Prayer, 144, 195, 209
Prescriptive, 42
Price, 127
Process, 9, 49, 59, 78, 99, 138,
  149, 177

Q
Quid-pro-quo, 113, 122

R
Rabbi, 22
Rank, 60
Reaction, 179
Responses, 94,115, 123
  Compliance, 125
  Commitment, 136
  Resistance, 124
Reciprocal, 9, 73, 78, 158
Responsibility, 20, 27, 37, 52,
  60, 139, 188, 196, 206
Resurrection, 22, 30, 83, 186
Rich Young Ruler, 25
Role, 90
Rost, Joseph, 72

S
Sanctification, 59, 95
Sanders, J. O., 134
Schein, Edgar, 169
Self-preservation, 71, 131, 207
Senge, Peter, 156
Senior Pastor, 112
Servant, 26
Servant Leadership, 153
Sheep, 27, 29, 39, 58, 146
Sheepness, 58
Sin, 75, 87, 118, 161, 179
Sine qua non, 99
Southern Baptist, 37
Stanley, Charles, 100
Status quo, 57, 76, 124
Stewardship, 115, 128, 180
Spears, Larry, 153
Structural freedom, 73
Subjugation, 114

Submission, 60, 90, 129, 132
  Illustration, 133
  Outcomes, 131
  Power, 161, 204, 129
Subordinates, 60
Subordination, 61
Suffering Servant, 26

T
Title, 87
Transactional Leader, 153
Transformational Leader, 151
Trials, 159
Trinity, 20, 21

U
Understanding, 173

W
Watson, G. D., 95
Webber, Max, 150
Well done, 31
Western Culture, 49
Whatever Followers, 76
Wholeness, 148
Winston, Bruce, 158
Wisdom, 173, 174
Worship, 44, 87
Worth, 21

About the Author

Dr. R. S. "Rusty" Ricketson is a much sought after speaker and teacher both nationally and internationally in the areas of leading/following and church growth. With a Bachelor of Social Science Education from the University of Georgia, a Master of Divinity degree from Southwestern Baptist Theological Seminary, a Doctor of Ministry degree from Reformed Theological Seminary, and a Ph.D. in Organizational Leadership from Regent University, Dr. Ricketson has a wide range of academic expertise. Coupled with over 30 years of ministry experience, including helping start two churches and serving as senior pastor for 18 years, Dr. Ricketson is able to blend academic insight with the practical application of one who has experienced ministry at the ground level. Dr. Ricketson is currently Associate Professor of Leadership at Luther Rice Seminary & University where he is the Chair of the Leadership Department, regularly teaching over 200 students per semester. Additionally, Dr. Ricketson serves as President of Foundation of the Faith, Inc., a ministry he founded in 2002 that is committed to developing followers of Christ to impact the world. With a dependence upon the Holy Spirit and an energetic and humorous approach, Dr. Ricketson facilitates learning and encourages those who hear him. He and his wife, Sharon, live north of Atlanta, Georgia with their two miniature dachshunds and golden retriever. They have two adult children.

Dr. Ricketson conducts half-day, full-day, and multiple-day workshops and consultations for churches, non-profit organizations, and businesses.

For more information contact:

www.followerfirst.com
www.foundationofthefaith.org

For your free copy of the Follower First Profile go to www.followerfirst.com and enter the code: 3208

NOTES

NOTES

NOTES

NOTES

NOTES

NOTES